MW01256159

What Others Are Saying
About Anne Garland and This Book

"Anne Garland gets it. She says out loud what many of us secretly think about networking: 'Ugh!'—and then teaches us, step-by-step, how to change that mindset and build connections, using empathy, humor, and stories that make it all stick. Have fun!"

— Randye Kaye, Actress and Author of *Happier Made Simple: Choose Your Words. Change Your Life.*

"Anne Garland's *Secrets of a Serial Networker* reads like you're in a cool convertible with your best friend, the wind blowing back your hair, the radio blasting foot-stomping tunes, and the journey as fun-filled as any destination could ever be. Anne delivers her networking secrets wrapped in delicious stories and humble truths of how she became the expert connector she is today. Ride along for the fun. Strap in for the wisdom."

— Robin Fox, M.Ed. and Author of *Social Eyes Together: Ignite the Power of Belonging*

"It's no secret that Anne Garland, a genuine and natural people magnet, over-delivers in her gem of a read, *Secrets of a Serial Networker: Connect, Serve and Attract More Clients*. She's charming and generous in person and on paper, and her new book is inspiring, informational, and hysterical. *Secrets of a Serial Networker* will have you laughing and thinking as you jot down all of Anne's tips and tricks for leveraging any networking scenario—whether you are the guest or the host of an event, and even if it's virtual. Anne provides incredibly useful real-world scripts to skyrocket any interaction. Get ready to elevate ordinary conversations into extraordinary possibilities. A remarkable read for anyone looking to boost their business and sales savvy in a fun and effective way."

— Audra Garling Mika, College Admissions Consultant, Career Development Coach

"With wit and humor, Anne Garland navigates you through the steps for becoming successful in building your centers of influence. *Secrets of a Serial Networker* gives you the guidance and tools you need to create a solid framework for building rapport and establishing trusting relationships with people who want to refer you. You'll learn, you'll laugh...and then you'll get to work meeting new friends."

— Michelle Jacobik, Business Profitability Strategist and Author of *Prosperity After Divorce* and *The Path to Profits*

"Anne Garland is a master when it comes to networking and making connections. Her natural tendency is to connect people and watch the sparks fly into mutual success. In her book, *Secrets of a Serial Networker*, Anne shares a step-by-step approach to effective networking, whether to support you in gaining employment, expanding your business, or simply finding a new group of amazing people to associate with. Expanding your circle, bringing joy into your life and the lives of others, and becoming comfortable in new settings are all simple with Anne's guidance. You've made a great choice in purchasing the life-long secrets she is sharing with you here. Enjoy the read!"

— Dorothy A. Martin-Neville, PhD, Speaker,
Coach, Consultant, and Author

"Anne Garland has written a must-read book for anyone who uses networking to grow their business. I've known Anne for more than ten years and have attended almost every event she has offered. Her warmth, style, and creativity make everyone who attends feel at ease. If networking scares you or bores you, you must read this book. It will change the way you network and build relationships. If nothing else, read the chapter 'What Does Men's Underwear Have to Do with Networking?' Hilarious!"

— Susan Epstein, Business Coach Strategist

"Anne Garland's networking tips are so brilliant that I wish I'd had this book years ago when I started networking! I first met Anne in 2009 at a networking event. At the end of the meeting, after hearing my elevator speech, she came over to me, introduced herself, and said, 'I want to meet you!' I was immediately drawn to her warmth, upbeat attitude, and professionalism as she recruited for her networking event. I was so happy to get to know Anne and soon learned that she was truly the queen of networking! I have learned so much from Anne by being part of her networking groups. Her book is an amazing guide to handling all those situations that make networking uncomfortable with very practical, easy ways to feel great while creating new relationships. The book is written in her voice, and her fun-loving, warm personality shines through with her personal stories that are easy to relate to. Anne always lights up a room when she enters and makes everyone she encounters feel important. This book will provide anyone willing to learn with all the tools needed to grow their businesses while creating their own network."

— Fern Tausig, Certified Hypnotist, Master Trainer at Healing Hypnosis and Life Coach

"Anne Garland's passion for making network connections, for women and men, but particularly for up-and-coming women entrepreneurs, is invaluable. Her book provides many useful and insightful tips that are so beneficial for relationship building. Anne's desire to lift others through education is genuine, and her book is the next best thing to working directly alongside her as you develop and hone your own networking skills.

Her life experiences and storytelling skills make this an enjoyable read! You can be assured there are tips in this book you can use in your own journey."

— Brenda L. McConnell, Founder and CEO of Green Wave Power Systems, LLC

"Move over Lucille Ball. Anne Garland is now my favorite redhead because her hilarious antics throughout her business career can actually help you learn how to make the connections you need to advance your business and help your newfound friends advance theirs. The chapter on how to approach people at a networking event is alone worth ten times the price of this book."

— Tyler R. Tichelaar, PhD and Award-Winning Author of *Narrow Lives* and *The Best Place*

"*Secrets of a Serial Networker* is a modern roadmap for navigating networking whether in person, virtually, or even when hosting your own networking events. Elegantly simple insights, immediately actionable tips, shared in Anne's brilliantly authentic style of compassion and humor will provide both the entrepreneur and the job seeker real-world guidance to connecting with people and building relationships. Packed with encouraging advice, whimsy, and wisdom, you will discover strategies that go beyond collecting business cards and turn networking into a profitable resource for your business and an opportunity to achieve more greatness in life when you learn to connect to serve."

— Janet Wise, MS HRD Corporate Learning Officer and Founder of The Branding Room

"Anne is the pro in the know. Take her advice and watch your world explode!"

— Leslie Singer, Actress, Artist, and Educator

"When I was in college, as a communications major I was in a group called WICI (Women in Communications, Inc.). We studied people like Anne. She's got a certain *je ne sais quoi* about her, you know—that essence that makes someone distinctive or attractive. It's that thing you want but can't descibe. It's unique. It's natural spontaneous truth! It's what every girl going through a communications program is seeking and aspires to be. Heck, it's what I want to be now that I'm an adult! Anne has a mentor quality that she doesn't even know she has... and *that* is what makes her so great! Anne is a woman to watch!"

— Nicole Gabriel, Podcast Host, Author of *Finding Your Inner Truth* and *Stepping Into Your Becoming*

"You must read this funny, inspiring, and informative book! Anne Garland is *the networker*, sharing, caring, and connecting. For twenty years, she has been the main source of my important contacts both personally, professionally, and through her extraordinary events. Her far-reaching skills and ideas sweep you into a great adventure."

— Chris Rigali, Former President
of Apparel Manufacturing

"Networking is that elusive goldmine we all want but find hard to discover. In *Secrets of a Serial Networker*, Anne Garland shows how you can strike gold by using the powerful strategies she offers to meet the right people to power your business and theirs. Creating your own destiny requires creating friends, and networking will allow you to do both. Take Anne's advice and watch your value and influence increase."

— Patrick Snow, Publishing Coach and
International Bestselling Author of *Creating
Your Own Destiny* and *Boy Entrepreneur*

"This book is *fun*. I loved the road stories and funny escapades. Helped me feel like I'm not the only one who's been awkward! Anne has so many valuable points. She's helped me realize the importance of 'getting to know you,' which I used to always rush before. I highly recommend this book for you and anyone who wants to succeed!"

— Elaine Williams, Video Coach,
Speaker Coach, Author, and Comedian

"Anne Garland's roadmap to making true networking connections is as entertaining and readable as it is powerful. Flowing from Rule #1: Never take yourself too seriously (refer to chicken on this cover), this guide contains nuggets for in-person and virtual networking that will both make you think and laugh out loud."

— Ellen Feldman Ornato, Founding Partner, Bolder Company Inc

"She's done it again! Anne has brilliantly and masterfully pulled together a lifetime collection of tips, tools, and tricks on networking that will educate and elevate your networking skills while keeping you in stitches! I have been witness to Anne in action…she is genuine, nonconventional, and surely *not* boring when it comes to networking and nurturing relationships in business and life. Always expect the unexpected from Anne Garland! Grab this book for yourself and your bestie!"

— Paula Jean Burns, Owner, RockPaperSistas, Guildford, Connecticut

"I fell in love with Anne the first time we met at a retreat for Entrepreneurs in Connecticut run by the wonderful Susan Epstein. What I learned from Anne at that first meeting continues to be true as our friendship and collaborations have deepened. She is authentically herself wherever she is and whatever she does. She personifies all that she teaches, but it doesn't feel like 'networking' when you are in her presence. You sense that she genuinely cares and you feel like the most important person in the world. She also had me laughing within minutes. Do yourself a favor and read this delightful book. You will learn the art of networking from a master *and* have a blast doing it. Although you may not have had the pleasure of meeting Anne in person, as I did, you will feel her beautiful, fiery light shining through every page, encouraging you to step into your best self and create lasting relationships that lead to raving fans."

— Monique McDonald,
The Magnetic Voice

"Anne Garland is the kind of person who, when you meet her, you instantly know you are talking with someone very, very special. It was that way for me. When I first met Anne, I immediately knew we were soul sisters, sharing the same values and vision for ourselves and our world. Anne is a spitfire, humorous, quick-witted, and successful entrepreneur who knows how to pivot when life isn't fun anymore and it's time to move on. Anne has this very special gift of seeing you as your future self. She will advocate for you, connect you, and introduce you to influential people who will propel you forward, even when you are scared and doubtful. Anne has a way of filling you up with courage as she guides you into growing with a new experience."

— Debbie Sodergren, Founder
& CEO of Up Vibrations, LLC

"I love *Secrets of a Serial Networker*! It's got a wonderful combination of humor and actionable tips. It has great ideas for newbie networkers as well as consummate pros—it's the perfect gift to share with friends!"

— Heather Hansen O'Neill, Author,
Speaker, and Behavioral Change Expert

"Anne Garland walked up to me at a conference and said, 'I need to know you.' I laughed, we chatted for a couple of minutes, exchanged cards, and parted ways. The next day she *phoned* me to invite me to an event. Who does that? A serial networker, that's who. Since then, we've become friends, shared connections, and driven business to one another. If you dread networking as much as I did, this book will become your bible. Annie's straightforward approach to creating connections that create connections is the most powerful thing you can add to your personal and professional toolkit."

— Wendy Perrotti, CPC Author, Speaker
Coach, and Founder of Live BIG

"I love Anne Garland, a fellow entrepreneur and a friend of many years. I love her energy, her positive attitude, and her sense of humor. And she is a smart gal...who offers advice with a big smile. It's not often in the business world of women that you meet someone like her, someone who endears herself into your mind and heart. She became someone I trusted when I decided to follow her, unquestioningly, into a new-to-our-area networking group, eWomen Network. No questions, just, where do I sign? When I heard she was writing *Secrets of a Serial Networker*, I was excited because she is *the* supreme networker and connector. This book is an elixir of her personality, positive spirit, intelligence, and vast experience. Most "to-do" books can be straight information, where you yawn as you turn to the next page. Not here. This book is a fun read, and you will learn some great ideas on how you can develop your business/career through networking...."

— Marilyn Wright Dayton, Entrepreneur, Novelist, and Creative Writer

"*Secrets of a Serial Networker* is the must-have playbook for anyone who needs to network! Anne's humor and unique storytelling style reveal her secrets from decades of being in the networking trenches. Even as a seasoned networker, I gained so many useful insights!"

— Deborah Daniel, CPA, Founder of Women's Wealth Secrets

"If the title hasn't grabbed you or the fabulous cover hasn't totally made you smile and wonder what could be fresh and new in networking, grab it now! Anne can tell a story like no one else. The way she weaves her amazing life experiences (some of which, I warn you, will cause you to belly-laugh) into life lessons is beyond creative. You will get so much out of this book and want to reach for it over and over, if not for the great reminders on how to network, share your story, and get out there, then for the entertaining stories! A must-read!"

— Lynn Gallant, Wellness & Lifestyle Educator

"Anne Garland's *Secrets of a Serial Networker* is a hilarious and heartfelt account of her rise from job-seeking newbie to the most well-connected businesswoman in her community. If you don't have the privilege of being in Anne's incredibly huge and warm network of fans, you will really enjoy getting a behind-the-curtain look at how she created her relationships and turned them into business success."

— Chala Dincoy, Marketing Strategist

"If you asked me who should write *Secrets of a Serial Networker*, only one name would come up: Anne Garland. Anne is the quintessential networking connector in our area. She has made international networking groups available to many of us who were too shy to seek them out. Everyone always feels welcome at the events Anne creates through her networking company. She has taken her in-person and virtual networking brilliance and written it down for you. If you are looking to network to improve your career or business, read this book!"

— Robin H. Clare, Best-Selling Author and Podcast Host of *Hungry for Answers*

"No one knows networking like Anne Garland. She has been connecting people for years. It comes so naturally to her and her willingness to help knows no bounds. Having known Anne for many, many years, I have seen her in action at many events, introducing people who might not have been comfortable in a setting of unfamiliar people. This book will be a great help in this new world where we cannot always meet in person. A definite must for your business library."

— Robin Lensi, Photographer, Lensi Designs

"Where was this book all my life? Anne Garland has over-delivered in *Secrets of a Serial Networker*. I wouldn't expect anything else. The first time I met Anne, I witnessed her ability to work the room to make people feel seen, heard, and (more importantly) connected. It was awe-inspiring. Anne works the room like magic, and I'm thrilled she's put her magic into a system for us all to learn her secrets. Anne has a heart of gold and knows her purpose is to connect people. She's built such deep relationships, and I'm honored to call her a friend. If you want to learn how to make authentic connections, make more money, and make an even bigger impact by networking, Anne Garland is the go-to expert. She's funny, thoughtful, and smart as a whip. As someone who's transacted well over a million dollars through networking and relationship building, I know I could have quadrupled that amount if I had known Anne's secrets to success. I'm recommending *Secrets of a Serial Networker* to every woman entrepreneur I know. I highly recommend you read this book now and put Anne's secrets into action for yourself."

— Terra Bohlmann, Business Strategist
for Women Entrepreneurs

"*Secrets of a Serial Networker* unveils the keys for successful networking. Anne is brilliant at guiding you to find your networking truth. Anne is equally talented at sharing her humorous struggles and tools to overcome and avoid uncomfortable situations. I am honored to be Anne's friend and can honestly say she knows how to command a room. She has a gift for connecting and making a person feel like the most interesting and important person in the room. There are many gems to take away from Anne's book."

— Sylvia Guinan, MBA, CDFA, Financial
Advisor, Author, and Speaker

"The fabulous picture of the author with a rubber chicken sets the tone for this wonderful book. Anne Garland describes how networking is like 'getting lost in the right direction.' You just know you're in great hands when it comes to networking, whether it's on-line or in person. If you've ever dreaded networking, as I have, you'll find this book to be a treasure trove of tips and tricks that take the fear out of networking. Anne Garland takes you gently by the hand and explains why you should network, and how to do it with grace. As you read, you will smile with curiosity, knowing 'the chicken crossed the road to meet other chicks'! Here's to happy and successful networking. Yes, networking can be fun when you learn how to do it the way Anne does!"

— Lynda Goldman, Author, Artist

"Anne Garland has an extraordinary ability to foresee connections with people. It is no surprise that she has created this powerful and fun book, sharing her experiences, gifts, and talents. Networking and connecting is an art, and Anne is the artist who paints a picture of how this can be done in a beautiful and authentic way. I highly recommend this book."

— Aina Hoskins, Author, Coach, and Executive Managing Director of eWomenNetwork, Connecticut Chapter

"Anne Garland has truly hit the mark with her incredible book, *Secrets of a Serial Networker*. Her humorous style and personal stories offer a powerful new way to build authentic connections and grow your client base. By sharing her years of extensive knowledge, tips, and tools for more heart-based connections, Anne shows how an authentic approach to networking creates a win-win situation for all involved! I loved her approach and highly recommend this book to every person growing a business or who simply desires to create community!"

— Astara Jane Ashley, CEO and
Publisher of Flower of Life Press

"Anne Garland is truly a master connector who shares not only her humor but her depth of knowledge when it comes to networking. As a Connections Strategist, I know how difficult it can be to navigate the networking world. Anne breaks it down into easy steps and turns the work of networking into something fun and enjoyable. As someone who has seen Anne in action working her networking magic, I know both introverts and extroverts looking to make the right connections and move forward in their businesses will want to read this book."

— Stephanie Arnheim, Connections
Strategist, Stephanie Connects

"Anne is the connector and networker you want to know and learn from. You can always 'expect the unexpected' as she brings humor, fun, and the honest truth to any conversation, and this is so true of her book. I chuckled as she shared her triumphs and tribulations, all the while learning about the importance of networking. And let's talk about the book cover! The unexpected, but it's beautifully tied into her message to put yourself out there and show the world who you really are. This is a book you will want to reference and reflect on repeatedly. Thanks for sharing your wisdom with the world, Anne!"

— Dena Otrin, Holistic Empowerment Coach
and Licensed Professional Counselor

"Oh, what fun it is to travel with Anne Garland as she takes you along on her journey to becoming a serial networker, sharing the juicy details and her secrets to success. Consider her your networking fairy godmother. Whether you're just starting your career, or you have years of experience, Anne's book will make you excited about getting out there and making new connections."

— Maureen Sullivan, President, Maureen Sullivan
Media, Founder of Girls Just Wanna Have Fun

"I have seen first-hand how Anne Garland works her networking magic at events. As someone who puts monthly events together, I really enjoyed 'The Magical Mystery Tour' that Anne guides us through, and that truly supports her reputation when it comes to details as you will read in Chapter 29. Visualizing your event from dream to reality is the magic ingredient that will create your perfect event every single time."

— Diane Trone, Owner Blonde Hanger/His Hanger Showroom in the Velvet Mill, Stonington, Connecticut

"From one fiery redhead to another, of course I was drawn to Anne immediately! Naturally, I met her through networking and mutual friends. Over the years, I have attended many of Anne's events as well as photographed her several times, and it's easy to say that no one connects people quite like Anne. Her intention is genuine and comes from the place that relationship building is key. Now Anne shares all her hard-earned expertise in *Secrets of a Serial Networker*. Anne really thrives on being a master connector, and I'm honored to be in her energy. Now you can experience that energy too!"

— Carrie Roseman, Photographer, Carrie Roseman Studio

"Anne Garland unpacks her decades of experience as a master networker in this witty, easy-to-read, and value-packed reference for anyone who wants to advance their career and have fun doing it."

— Robin Colucci, CEO, R Colucci, LLC

"Anne Garland takes the mystery out of networking, creating a blueprint for leaving a positive imprint on strangers. *Secrets of a Serial Networker* is a resource for making us all more self-aware and strategic when interacting with others."

— Pat Lore, TV Host, Author, and Video Producer

"*The Secrets of a Serial Networker* is chock-full of practical wisdom and actionable tips to help you build meaningful relationships and connections both professionally and personally. It highlights essential communication skills you need to expand your networking comfort zone to have richer and less awkward interactions."

— Susan Friedmann, CSP and Bestselling
Author of *Riches in Niches: How to Make
it BIG in a small Market*

"Everything is who you know and perfect timing. We can't control time, but we can control who we know. Connecting with Anne Garland is a power move for anyone looking to expand their network, visibility, and ROI. This book is a valuable resource to reference often because it offers a trifecta of genius insight into the networking world. Be a curious chicken who dares to cross the road. Your people are waiting for you!"

— Ashley Roda, CEO, Iconic Details

"*Secrets of a Serial Networker* is a must read for those who want to create wonderful futures and need guidance on how to do it with joy, trust, and humor. Anne clearly maps out the importance of creating and building relationships but also the great impact of doing it consciously and in service. Read this book, and you too can be in the right place at the right time and create the future you have always dreamed of which is exactly where you want to be. Anne is truly one of the most brilliant, generous, and thoughtful women I have had the honor and delight to have in my circle. She is selfless in her service for having people succeed, and she walks her talk."

— Deborah Stuart CEO, High Chi Energy Jewelry

"Anne is an engaging author and finds a way to inject humor into a topic that usually fills me and many others with dread: networking! I read Anne's chapters in previous books, including the *Be the Beacon* anthology. She was masterful in sharing her message in those books, so I was intrigued to get her take on networking in her new book. Needless to say, I was not disappointed! This book hits all the points we all need to know about in-person networking, virtual networking, which is so important nowadays, and of course, creating our own networking events. If you are looking for exactly how to network in an authentic way, this is your primer!"

— Dr. Davia H. Shepherd, Author of *Grow Smarter*

"Anne Garland is like having your very own networking sherpa with a wild sense of humor. She has brilliantly compiled her years of successful networking into an easy-to-follow guide that will show even the most reserved introvert how to build their business as they create relationships that will last a lifetime."

— Felicia Searcey, Results Expert

"I am an extrovert and love people, but that doesn't mean I understand networking. But I don't need to because I am fortunate to know Anne Garland and she is the master. With a background in event planning, she knows what works, so when she speaks, I pay attention, and you should too! This book is a treasure trove of wisdom, great ideas, and methods to get you focused on other people, which makes you a social magnet. Anne's techniques are refreshingly bold and full of sincerity rather than selfish sales tactics. She is a true leader with a servant's heart, which is why she was elected as President of the Connecticut Chapter of the National Speakers Association. So grab your rubber chicken and get into Anne's parade for networking victory!"

— Curt Vincent, Principal,
Cyber Assurance Associates

"*Secrets of a Serial Networker* will get you thinking differently about networking. Networking, for many, can be the 'death' of them, but for most, networking is what pays the bills. Anne brings her delightful insights into the networking world. She speaks her truth about what it means to network, and she brilliantly ties together her own personal stories with her own networking experiences. I absolutely love how she isn't afraid to share some of her more personal stories that will make you laugh! This book is for you: someone who avoids or is scared of networking. Anne helps to relieve this burden by letting you read about her own world of networking. As you read, I know you will receive the same benefit I did—the ability to let go of your fear of a very important role in life—networking."

— Jonathan Bengal, Founder of JB Financial LLC
and Naked Tax Talk LLC

"Anne Garland is The Connector and Networker you want to know and learn from. You can always 'expect the unexpected' from her as she brings humor, fun, and the honest truth to any conversation, and this is so true of her book. I chuckled when reading passages as she shares her triumphs and tribulations, and all the while, I learned about the importance of networking. And let's talk about the book cover! The unexpected, but it's beautifully tied into her message to put yourself out there and show the world who you really are. This is a book you will want in your repertoire to reference and to reflect upon how to be a successful networker. Thanks for sharing your wisdom with the world, Anne!"

— Dena Otrin, LPC, Bayside Counseling

SECRETS
OF A SERIAL NETWORKER

CONNECT,
SERVE,
AND
ATTRACT
MORE
CLIENTS

ATTRACTING YOUR IDEAL PROSPECTS FOR DEEPER
CONNECTIONS AND GREATER PROFITS

ANNE GARLAND

FOREWORD BY
SANDRA YANCEY,
CEO and Founder, eWomenNetwork

AVIVA
PUBLISHING
New York

SECRETS OF A SERIAL NETWORKER

CONNECT, SERVE, AND ATTRACT MORE CLIENTS

Attracting Your Ideal Prospects for Deeper Connections and Greater Profits

AVIVA
PUBLISHING
New York

Copyright © 2022 by Anne Garland
All rights reserved.
Published by:
Aviva Publishing
Lake Placid, NY
(518) 523-1320
www.AvivaPubs.com

All Rights Reserved. No part of this book may be used or reproduced in any manner whatsoever without the expressed written permission of the author. Address all inquiries to:

Anne Garland
(860) 575-4970
Anneg@AnneGarlandEnterprises.com
www.SecretsofaSerialNetworker.com
www.AnneGarlandEnterprises.com

ISBN: 978-1-63618-163-9 (hard cover)
          978-1-63618-172-1 (ebook)
Library of Congress Control Number: 2021924584

Editors: Tyler Tichelaar and Larry Alexander, Superior Book Productions
Cover Designer: Nicole Gabriel, Angel Dog Productions
Interior Book Layout: Nicole Gabriel, Angel Dog Productions
Author Photo: Carrie Roseman Studios

Every attempt has been made to properly source all quotes.
Printed in the United States of America
First Edition

2 4 6 8 10 12

DEDICATION

To all of the connections I have made during my lifetime who have fueled my networking journey.

And to my true love and husband, Keith, who is amazingly patient and supportive and gives me balance. I give him imbalance.

"Networking is the number-one unwritten rule of success in business."

— Sally Krawcheck, author, power woman, speaker

ACKNOWLEDGMENTS

Writing *Secrets of a Serial Networker* has been an interesting retrospective ride across the many highways of my life, potholes included. I have traveled meeting thousands of people over the decades. And if not for them, I wouldn't be here and neither would you be reading this book.

Truth be told, I had a rough start getting this book to paper early on when I hired my first book coach at a time when I had taken on too many obligations. I crashed and burned. However, the seed was planted even if it went dormant. Then, beautiful Astara Jane Ashley, sweet goddess that she is, revived me from the ashes, encouraging me to get this book out there. That was another short-lived start and stop due to a chaotic 2020.

Audra Garling Mika, a sometimes editor for selective clients who I am lucky to have on speed dial for quick editing therapy, is a brilliant writer with sensitivity. I owe her more gratitude than I can give here. When chaos shook our world in the spring of 2020 and in-person networking went silent, I did too. I then wanted to write a short book about virtual networking, and Audra entered my life, and soon after, so did Patrick Snow.

I've learned it takes a village to produce a book. I

am filled with tremendous gratitude for my *Secrets of a Serial Networker* A-Team, and want to thank the following.

The first and biggest secret I will share in this epic endeavor is the incredible team of people I've enlisted. Actually, it was Patrick Snow my (always on my butt) *final* book coach who enlisted the team to make this book truly come to life. Thank you, Patrick, for believing I should finish this book and that it had nothing to do about scoring a fee. Patrick got me writing again. Even though the cover usually comes later in the process, I wanted to take my inspiration and see it in print. Patrick had me first call Nicole Gabriel to the team. She was the most amazing woman for creating my vision of the cover, and later made magic with her creative book layout—a thousand thanks, Nicole. I always enjoyed our conversations beyond the book and hope they continue. During this process, I had a blow-up copy of the book cover sitting on my desk with a chicken, seemingly screaming with raucous cackling, reminding me daily to get this book done. Thanks to Carrie Roseman Studios and her professional team—Keely Lozier, wardrobe stylist, and Miranda Lynn Berube, hair and makeup—for the fun photo shoot capturing Dixie, the chicken (I did name her) and me with feathers flying with laughter that I chose for the cover! Fun for sure! A special thank you to Tyler Tichelaar, a masterful editor who I believe I may have made smile a few times with his "funny" in quote side comments while editing, often suggesting sage advice which I happily embraced. Larry Alexander who partnered with Tyler injected his skill and knowledge as well. Next, Patrick wanted me to meet my publisher, a delightful Englishwoman with wonderful charm and a smart head for business and marketing, Susan Friedmann, Aviva Publishing. She, like Patrick, had a magic key for opening doors I would have never opened otherwise. I also want to thank Ryan Seidner at Baker & Taylor, my printer, for bringing the words to a three-dimensional format and finding enough paper in a shortage; it's always something!

There is another team that has been by my side even before the book moved into advanced stages for whom I am supremely grateful. Troy Van Marter keeps me in check with tech. My whip smart Generation Z virtual assistant Karoline Kujawa makes magic with all things social media and so much more. Teri Prestash, whom I met at a networking meeting and told then we would be working together. It was just a feeling, but two years later, I called her, and it's been a "graphics/branding" love affair ever since. She is awesome! My dedicated, reliable bookkeeper, Laura Holcomb, keeps me fiscally straight. And my adorable housekeeper, Lindsay Clark, saves me so much time. I couldn't do what I do in business without them. They, too, keep me balanced so I could write this book.

There are so many more people I want to thank, who have supported me in some way with this book and continue to support me in life. I want each of you listed to know you are etched deeply in my heart for impacting my life in more ways than I can profess here. I am a better person for knowing each of you. So not to make this segment its own book, I will list only your names...in Pig Latin. Just kidding!

To all of you in deep gratitude: Astara Jane Ashley, Jonathan Bengal, Terra Bohlmann, Paula Burns, Robin Clare, Robin Colucci, Nancy Cohen, Briana Dai, Marilyn Dayton, Liz Dederer, Chala Dincoy, Susan Epstein, Robin Fox, Lynn Gallant, Lynda Goldman, Sylvia Guinan, Heather Hanson O'Neill, Aina Hoskins, Michelle Jacobik, Janine James, Randye Kaye, Kathy Keegan, Robin Lensi, Pat Lore, Dr. Dorothy Martin-Neville, Brenda McConnell, Monique McDonald, Dr. Maura McQueeney, Ellen Feldman Ornato, Dena Otrin, Wendy Perrotti, Chris Rigali, Felicia Searcey, Dr. Davia Shepherd, Leslie Singer, Debbie Merrick Sodergren, Loretta Stevens, Deborah Stuart, Maureen Sullivan, Fern Tausig, Diane Trone, Sally Tucker, Curt Vincent, Elaine Williams, Janet Wise, Kym Yancey, and Sandra Yancey.

Finally, to the true loves of my life, my husband

Keith; my daughter Lauren and family, Sam, Orson, and Wild; and my son John, and family, Ann, Virgil, and Alma. They bring me the greatest joy I've ever known.

Oh! I almost forgot, Dixie the Chick on the cover—thanks for all the laughs!

*"Networking is about knowing more people.
Connecting is about knowing people more."*

— Author unknown

CONTENTS

Preface   41

Foreword   45

Introduction: When Networking Is Not Work-   51
         ing for You

**SECTION ONE In-Person Networking: "You   57
Had Me at Hello"**

Chapter 1   Building Relationships Before   59
               You Need Them

Chapter 2   A Referral Story from a Road   67
               Warrior

Chapter 3   What Does Men's Underwear   81
               Have to Do with Networking?

Chapter 4   Making a Lasting First Impres-   91
               sion: "You Had Me at Hello"

Chapter 5   Mapping Out Your Gold Mine   105

Chapter 6   Selling Yourself Is an Art   111

Chapter 7   Expand Your Circle of Influence   143

Chapter 8   Mining for Gold   151

Chapter 9   Digging in the Mine—Going   161
               Deeper

Chapter 10 Following the Gold: Discover-   169
               ing the True Secret of a Serial
               Networker

Chapter 11   Securing Your Gold   175

Chapter 12   It's a Wrap: We Have Been Doing Networking All Wrong!   183

SECTION TWO Split Second Connections: Thirty Worthy Tips for Making the Most of Virtual Networking   **187**

Introduction: A Brave New World—Virtual Networking   189

Chapter 13   Adjusting to a Brave New World, the Now of Networking   195

Chapter 14   Why Virtual Networking Is So Vital   199

Chapter 15   Mastering Your Square from the Tech Perspective   205

Chapter 16   Mastering Your Square to Be Visible Virtually   211

Chapter 17   Getting Personal Online: Netiquette   217

Chapter 18   Making Connections Virtually Is Easier than In-Person   227

Chapter 19   Follow-Up in a Virtual World   231

Chapter 20   It's a Wrap! Virtual or In-Person?   235

SECTION THREE Networking with a Twist: 237
    Creating Networking Events
    Where You Are the Star!

Introduction: My Unexpected Journey as an   239
     Event Producer

Chapter 21 Creating Networking Events   251
     Where You Are the Star!

Chapter 22 Planning a Successful Networking   255
     Event: Determine Your Goal

Chapter 23 What's in It for Them?   259

Chapter 24 It's All in the Details!   263

Chapter 25 Networking at Events   273

Chapter 26 What Is the Takeaway?   279

Chapter 27 Show Me the Money!   285

Chapter 28 Plan-Do-Review   289

Chapter 29 A Magical Mystery Tour   295
     Experience

Chapter 30 It's A Wrap! Your Time Is NOW!   307

A Final Note Connecting, Serving, and   311
Attracting More Clients

SPECIAL REPORTS AND RESOURCES   **317**

1. How Charismatic Are YOU? Take the   319
  Quiz

2. Anne's Plan-Do-Review: 20 Quick Steps for a Successful Networking Event   329

3. Resources for Download   333

4. Anne's List of Favorite Quotes   335

5. Anne's "A List" of VIP Resources   347

6. About Spotlight Coaching   351

7. About Wing Woman Coaching   355

8. About the Author   357

9. About Anne Garland Enterprises, LLC   361

10. Book Anne Garland to Speak at Your Next Event   369

"No one makes it alone."

— Anne Garland, author, speaker, master connector

PREFACE

I was wrapping up this book in February 2020, or so I thought, when uncertainty and challenges rocked the world we knew. It was evident I could no longer address only in-person networking when I witnessed so many people struggling to effectively network online with Zoom and other social media platforms. I paused my book because it was evident that in-person anything would not be happening anytime soon.

I immediately shifted my focus to include important tips to help navigate networking online.

This book is now divided into three sections to offer you universal networking insights and tips as well as suggestions specific to connecting either virtually or in-person. Think of it as three books in one.

Throughout these pages, you will find solutions to master each situation with confidence and ease.

Section One: In-Person Networking: "You Had Me at Hello"

Section Two: Split Second Connections: Thirty Worthy Tips to Make the Most of Virtual Networking

Section Three: Networking with a Twist: Creating In-Person Networking Events Where *You* Are the Star!

However you choose to navigate my offerings, I am confident you will enjoy a few tasty bites that are satisfying with a dash of fun. I'm all about fun!

So, *why did* the chicken cross the road?

The chicken crossed the road…to meet other chicks!

It's the choice of risk vs. reward: the fear of not crossing vs. the fear of being left out or behind.

I don't want you to be either.

Blessings,

Anne Garland

Anne Garland
Author, Speaker, and Master Connector

P.S. I pronounce it "Annie"!

"Networking is a lot like nutrition and fitness: we know what to do. The hard part is making it a top priority."

— Herminia Ibarra, professor, London Business School

FOREWORD

By Sandra Yancey

Founder and CEO of eWomenNetwork

I had humble beginnings as a first-generation American. I lost my dad on my fifth birthday, and my mom became my guide and mentor while I was growing up. She was a strong and wise woman who played a large part in who I am today as I carry her legacy as a femtor (female mentor) and inspire women worldwide.

I began my career as a solopreneur when my husband and I moved to Dallas, Texas, from Ohio. I left my position as a manager for a Fortune 500 company and started my own consulting business with some big-named companies you would recognize today. I was set up in a spare room above our garage, working long hours. It didn't take long before I figured out that all I really did was create a job, only now with no paid vacation, no healthcare, and no time off, while struggling to raise our very young children with a husband working full-time. I was exhausted!

Then I began to ask, "Why am I struggling alone?" I

needed connections. I wanted to meet women who had the same financial drive and ambition as I did and who could help me see my blind spots. I found myself trying to network, but I couldn't find the right fit because most organizations were primarily men with few women. So, I started my own networking company in the year 2000, eWomenNetwork.

I founded the first chapter in Dallas, and soon after, someone from Atlanta, Georgia, heard about it and our second chapter was born. From there, eWomenNetwork grew slowly, but then gained momentum with chapters all across the United States and Canada. It wasn't easy, but with a great team and perseverance, today eWomenNetwork is a global multimillion-dollar business connected to more than 500,000 women (and yes, even men) business owners.

To what do I owe my company's success? What I discovered is the importance of a team and your capital is your relationships! I also discovered the importance of having a coach to succeed in business, how critical it is to always be learning from people smarter than me, how a network is essential for solving problems and thinking through opportunities, and how it is fueled through the relationships of those who are a part of a like-minded community.

Successful people, despite busy schedules, must invest in their own learning, stay innovative, and prioritize what's most significant in their life and business. In mine, it's the relationships that have propelled me to success.

One of those relationships has been with Anne Garland. I met Anne when she attended a New Jersey chapter meeting in the spring of 2014. Anne had stepped down from her thirty-five-year corporate career and was looking for her next big move. We saw something special in Anne that fit our leadership model.

We recruited her to join our team as a managing director to start an eWomenNetwork Chapter in Connecticut. She had been producing events for women as a side gig for years, so she had developed an impressive list of connections throughout Connecticut and the surrounding states.

It was a match made in heaven. She fell in love with us, and we fell in love with her.

Anne's strong leadership and people skills pulled together a powerful leadership team that enabled her to grow the chapter to one hundred members in nine months, making it one of the fastest-growing chapters in our history. That moved her up to an executive managing director position. We then elected her to our advisory board. Anne achieved many awards in her four years in these positions, and if you ask her which is the most important of all of those awards, it would be her Foundation Advocate Award because her heart is in giving back to the community.

Although Anne has passed the baton in leading the Connecticut chapter to a worthy successor, she is still very active as an important member of our eWomen-Network community.

In this powerful book, you will have a front seat to observe how Anne's success came from decades of building relationships. Anytime she had to pivot, there was a person and a referral to help her on her journey. Her lightheartedness will shine through, giving you, the reader, a ride like no other networking book you will ever read.

In Secrets of a Serial Networker, Anne will provide you with an easy-to-follow blueprint that will help you understand the three key reasons most people don't like to network and how you can put her practical and proven success tips into practice. When you follow her tips and strategies, you'll discover how easily a connection can be made, and as you begin to build and nurture this meaningful relationship, you will learn how it can develop into a long-lasting and valuable person in your network. As a bonus, in Section Three, Anne will share her secret sauce when it comes to creating and producing your own networking events, which have brought her acclaim and success for years.

Throughout this book, you will learn that you are the driver to becoming a masterful networker. Let Anne Garland be the driving force that assists you.

So, get ready for a fun and fantastic ride. Buckle up!

Sandra Yancey

Sandra Yancey is an award-winning entrepreneur, international business owner, transformation expert on The Doctors syndicated TV show, author, movie producer, speaker, and philanthropist dedicated to helping women achieve and succeed. She is the founder & CEO of eWomenNetwork, the number-one resource for connecting and promoting women and their businesses worldwide.

"The opposite of networking is NOT working!"

— Someone Smart

INTRODUCTION
WHEN NETWORKING IS NOT WORKING FOR YOU

Have you ever found yourself saying:

"Networking—Ugh! I hate networking! Why bother?"

You feel you don't get anything out of networking. You don't know how to approach someone, and you don't know what to say when you do. When someone does approach you, they are pushing their product or services, and it feels icky and "salesy" like used car salesman energy! You don't like talking about yourself to strangers. At most network meetings, the food is average, limited, and overpriced. Attending such meetings is a waste of time. If it weren't a business obligation, you wouldn't do it. You find the attendees are mostly all men, or mostly all women. You never meet anyone interesting. You hate people pushing their business cards on you. And you never follow up anyway because you don't know what to say when you do, or you don't have the time to follow up. Mostly, you don't like selling yourself to people. You hate networking! Ugh!

Sound familiar? You're not alone.

Yes, and...if it's a virtual meeting, you have to worry about the lighting, backdrop, sound, and your appearance. You're not that good at tech issues when something goes wrong. You have no privacy at home to feel professional when in a Zoom meeting. It's either the kids interrupting or the dog barking. You don't feel you have anything to contribute, so you stay quiet and listen. Perhaps you are an introvert and feel intimidated by the masses. You turn off your photo or name so no one can see you. Or you are an extrovert and tired of Zoom meetings. You prefer in-person meetings because it's difficult to be noticed in a tiny square...and on and on.

Whether you work for a big company or a small one, or you are an entrepreneur by choice or circumstance, you still need to market and promote yourself and your company in some capacity.

If you are currently unemployed and seeking employment, networking is more important now than ever, and I can help.

You will be pleased to know that networking does not come naturally to most people. Many people would rather have a root canal than walk into a room full of strangers.

News flash!

Yes, I'm a serial networker. Connecting and networking have always been second nature to me. However, put me in a room with no one I know, and I, too, can find that daunting. Yet I have learned how to overcome the uneasiness through years of trial and error. And I have tracked my secrets—all of which I will be sharing with you. Networking is like building a muscle. The more you use it correctly, the stronger it gets.

This book is not intended to be a typical how-to networking manual. It is designed to be more of a light-hearted view of my tips, insights, and stories, reflecting more than five decades of my life experiences. I have been there and back, and I know what works.

Growing up, people considered me fearless and bold. Those qualities likely came from my being the youngest of five children, with my eldest brother ten years older and my sister eight years older. I also had two other brothers who were six and four years older than I was. It was an unexpected surprise when I came along. As a scrappy, resourceful survivor, I felt growing up was like jumping out of an airplane and building wings to fly on my way down.

I have survived, and I always seem to land in the right place at the right time. I'm not sure whether it's been faith or serendipity, but I mostly feel I have good luck on my side. Before GPS, when I would travel in unfamiliar cities for business, I would joke that, somehow, I got lost in the right direction so I could find my way to my destination.

I am writing this book to share some of that luck with you. Maybe it's confidence you are seeking, or, perhaps it's belly laughs you seek from some of the *I Love Lucy* situations I got myself into along my networking journey. No matter why you are reading my book, I hope you will discover many gold nuggets you can use to build more self-confidence as you develop deeper connections. I want you to have greater visibility and make your cash register ring through greater serving.

Isn't that the goal of networking?

Today, hundreds of networking books are available that are full of statistics and graphs reflecting a corporate perspective. I've been in the corporate world most of my work life. I've always approached networking with a sense of fun because I seek to reap the benefits of the relationships I've built and nurtured over a lifetime. And my purpose in maintaining those relationships is always to serve people, never to sell, even though I have held professional "sales" positions.

In this book, my intention is to have you look at the lighter side of networking. I placed the "rubber chicken" on the cover to help prepare you to tap into the humor and fun of networking. I suspect you even smiled with some curiosity when you first saw the cover. Remember that feeling when you network and meet someone new. Smile with curiosity, knowing the chicken crossed the road to meet other chicks! Just like the chicks, you are tired of being cooped up. We can all relate to that, especially after all the uncertainty and drama we've all experienced over the last several years.

#networkingissmilingwithcuriosity

That's just the beginning of a few more smiles and secrets I hope to inspire.

So let's get started.

SECTION ONE

IN-PERSON NETWORKING: "YOU HAD ME AT HELLO"

"The richest people in the world look for and build networks. Everyone else looks for a job."

— Robert Kiyosaki, author of *Rich Dad Poor Dad*

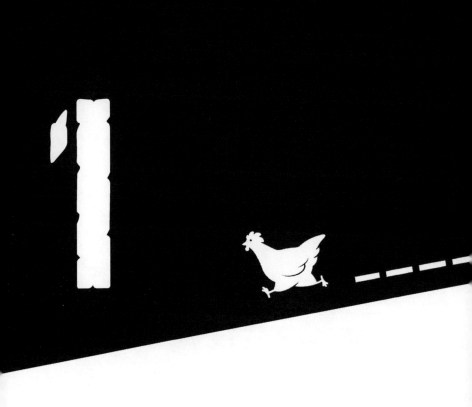

1

"You can make more friends in two months by becoming more interested in other people than you can in two years by trying to have them become interested in you."

— Dale Carnegie, American writer, lecturer

CHAPTER 1

BUILDING RELATIONSHIPS BEFORE YOU NEED THEM

Think back to a time when you moved into a new neighborhood. If you had kids, you had to meet with the school and get them enrolled. Then you may have had to find service providers, doctors, dentists, a pharmacy, a veterinarian, and all the other services to get you and your family set up in your new environment. You may have looked into the community for a place of worship, a grocery store, and a gym. I bet you even met a few of your neighbors while moving in.

The move may have been overwhelming, yet you pushed through, and you made some critical connections in the process. Some of those connections may have offered suggestions to help you find the best resources for organizing your new life in your new neighborhood.

Guess what? You were *building relationships before you needed them*.

I also presume when you found a great resource, you had no problem sharing your newfound connections with others who could use their services. That's called a referral.

Networking in business and life is connecting with people who have contacts to connect you to people who need to know you.

Unless you live in a bubble, you've had countless opportunities to socialize and meet people at events, parties, conferences, luncheons, Rotary, chamber events, and the like. Those attendees are there to grow their businesses just like you.

Why Networking Works for Some and Not for Others

Here's the "why" it works for some: The people most successful at getting new business by networking are *not* pitching their products and/or services. It is *not* about seeing dollar signs whenever you say, "Hello, what do you do?" It's *not* about me, me, me, and what you can do for *me*. This mindset is the most enormous red flag—one that a blind person can see. People who talk only about themselves and what they need and never ask about you, what drives you, or how they can help you are selfish, and they will never succeed at networking. Indeed, their failure to ask will jeopardize their profits and ongoing business relationships—more on this in a later chapter.

I have always said that people do business with people they know, like, and trust. You have heard this ad nauseam. If you re-engineer that statement, the simple truth is that a person can't *trust* you until they *like* you, and they can't *like* you until they *know* you. It's that simple.

Successful networking is about give-and-take conversations, building rapport, and establishing trusting relationships with people who want to refer you. When they fall in *like* with you and trust you, they will talk about you because they know you. They will talk about how great you are to work with and recommend you to their peers and contacts who are in need of your services or products.

Guess what? Some may never buy from you. Their help will usually come in the form of a referral. I call these referral people your raving fans, your supporters. A personal referral is the best marketing for any business; it is priceless, and no amount of money can buy its power.

This is so important that I want to repeat it:

A personal referral is the best marketing for any business; it is priceless, and no amount of money can buy its power.

A supporter or raving fan will sell *you* and bring you several clients, where a prospect (potential customer) may never become a sale.

I call a prospect a potential customer, which could translate as throwing darts blindfolded. The board is in front of you, and you are aiming, but you are often wasting your time.

I have proven time and again that building a relationship first through rapport is the best way to network, and the dividends are *big*.

This positive mindset takes the pressure off of you—you're not selling—and takes the pressure off the other person—neither of you sees the other as just a dollar sign. It's a comfortable win-win for all.

The "about me, me, it's all about *me*" theory proves that people who focus on themselves while networking fail when engaging with others.

My next theory is called the "give to get." This

mentality is better described as, "If I give you this, what will you give me?" Or, "If I do this for you, what will you do for me?" Ugh! This is when pitching and selling become icky.

If you offer a document, referral, book, small gift, or anything, please do so graciously and with no expectations. Give from the heart—when you give, when you lead from your heart and soul, you leave a powerful *emotional* imprint! That tells others you value them, and it makes a lasting impression.

I have built my reputation on giving, and it has come back a thousandfold. I receive calls and requests all the time from people who ask me, "Do you know someone who can help me with…?" I happily go into my contacts and share with no questions asked—and no expectations either. That is one way I have built a reputation for being a connector. Sometimes, I do suggest the person mention my name to the resource to create a warmer connection, still with no expectations. Other times, I will make the connection personally for them.

Networking is all about building relationships, not selling. It's about the personal connection, not business card collecting.

It's not what you know; it's who you know, who

they know, and how you can build rapport and help each other. That is where the magic is.

My good friend, Sally Tucker, is one of the best real estate agents in Connecticut. I watched Sally turn her struggling start-up business into a thriving, award-winning one in a short time. The next time I buy or sell a house, Sally will be the first person I will call or recommend—not because she is a friend, but because I know her ethics, heart, and personal drive to serve her customers beyond their expectations. I trust Sally. I know she will deliver.

Everyone in real estate will tell you the field can be profitable; however, selling is tricky, and you need to build a solid client base. That base is what all entrepreneurs and companies work to create. A client base is also known as a lead list. In this book, I'll help you learn how to build and track that lead list for better follow-up and greater profits.

#ServeNotSell

"Oh, the places you'll go!"

— Dr. Seuss, children's author

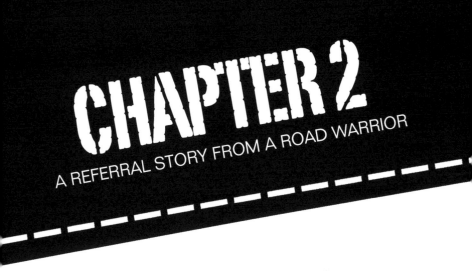

CHAPTER 2

A REFERRAL STORY FROM A ROAD WARRIOR

he early 1970s were tough. Many people struggled to find a job given the poor economy, high inflation rates, oil crisis, and gas shortages. Peasant shirts and homemade tie-dye became the rage while the economy was tanking.

The only real growth was high unemployment and men's facial hair. Heck, interest rates soared to 20 percent, while ladies' hemlines dropped 75 percent! Those crazy hippies!

We queued up at gas stations to wait in long lines, sometimes an hour or more, hoping gas didn't sell out before our turn at the pump. Notice any similarity to today?

I was even laid off from my enviable on-the-road sales rep position with Yardley of London. My job was to be a cheerful face and voice while schmoozing and promoting their cosmetic lines. Yardley began manufacturing soaps and perfumes such as English Lavender, which was considered an old lady perfume, before shifting to a new brand image of trendy Carnaby Street cosmetics with Twiggy and Jean Shrimpton as brand icons. Twiggy and Jean were both high-fashioned London models for branding in magazines and TV commercials. Needless to say, I loved my job! Very fun and exciting. I felt lucky.

I covered the East Coast, but I spent most of my time in the Northeast, specifically Connecticut and Massachusetts.

I recall a few road warrior stories, like when I set my bedsheets on fire in a Sheraton hotel outside of Boston. Not all hotels had irons, so I traveled with my portable one, just in case. Of course, often an ironing board was in short supply too, so I would either put a towel on the floor and iron there or pull back the blankets and iron on the sheets, being careful not to set the iron flat on the sheets to burn!

Often, I would dine alone in my hotel room to avoid being hit on by men staying at the hotels. That's a whole other story—maybe another book.

So, there I was one morning, carefully ironing away, when room service knocked at the door; I quickly let the waiter in, showing him where to put the tray. In that instant, I saw fear in his eyes, and he let out a yell. I quickly turned around to see the sheets had burst into flames. I ran to smother the fire with the bedspread and pull the plug on the iron.

Apparently, the cheap portable iron had gotten so hot that it had bubbled and melted the heel to stand the iron up and ignited the sheets.

Smoke, fire alarms, and fire trucks became part of my morning excitement. I moved to a new room. Ugh! I was so embarrassed. I'm surprised they let me stay another night. The staff addressed me as "the fiery redhead."

I subsequently had *all* food delivered to my room during the rest of my stay.

Today, I do not own a travel iron. I make it a habit of checking hotels to make sure they have ironing boards and irons. The little pleasures in life!

Another time, another Sheraton, I was in Braintree, Massachusetts, where my boss lived with his family. I headed out in the morning to meet him for breakfast so we could schedule calls to make together that day. As I walked out of the hotel's front entrance, a man stopped me to ask the time.

I looked at my watch, gave him the time, and he thanked me. I headed to my car.

While maneuvering my car in the parking lot, searching for the exit, I heard loud sirens, several of them. Looking to see where they were, I saw four police cars surrounding *my* car!

What the...?

The police got out of their vehicles and approached me, asking me to step out of my car. I didn't see any guns pointing at me—not that I could notice since I was a bit jarred by what was unfolding. They asked about my relationship with the man I had spoken to as I exited the hotel. I was able to explain clearly that I had only given him the time, and they let me go. It was quite the breakfast story when I met up late and a bit frazzled with my boss.

Ah, road stories...but wait, one more Yardley story.

I was called to work at the Yardley counter in Macy's cosmetic department in New Haven, Connecticut, back when it was a thriving mall store, to promote Yardley's newest perfume, "You're the Fire." (No pun intended.)

As women entered from the mall, I served as the first point of contact. I sprayed a sample of this lovely new fragrance in the air and on every woman who walked in to promote the brand and help with sales. Smart marketing. It worked. We sold a lot of perfume!

That afternoon, as I was leaving the store, I noticed I was slurring my words. I felt my tongue start to swell. I realized right away that I was having an allergic reaction to excessive inhalation of the perfume spray, and I did not feel well.

In my car heading to my hotel, I saw signs for the hospital. I decided I should check into the emergency room. I could barely talk.

The doctor started to psychoanalyze and dismiss me. He only suggested that I take over-the-counter Benadryl and stop spraying perfume. I could figure that out.

The following day, I wasn't much better, so I packed up and headed back home to New York State. I still couldn't speak very well. It was interesting when I called my boss; he actually thought I was drunk. But when I explained the problem, we fell into hysterics because I sounded so funny.

To this day, I cannot tolerate any aerosol sprays around me. When I start to feel my tongue tingle, I know trouble is growing, and so is my tongue!

Another aspect of my job responsibilities included replacing returns at the stores that carried Yardley products and taking fill-in orders. Monthly, I received a shipment from headquarters to restock my trunk with makeup, perfume products, and samples. My friends, who were always begging for samples, envied me. It was a fun and rewarding opportunity that helped pave my way to more sales opportunities.

Unfortunately, no job was safe in that economy. Soon I, too, had to give up not only my expense account that paid for my gas but, more importantly, my company car, a hot red Pontiac Firebird that my hip manager had ordered for me one month into the job. He thought, as a fiery redhead, I would look great in it. I sure felt great in it. I loved my car and the many perks that came with the job.

Naturally, facing the stark reality of needing new employment, the next step was to network with friends to find leads. However, most of what I found came from the newspapers or employment agencies.

At the time, I went on unemployment and was just scraping by. I thought to myself, *Before I apply at a McDonald's or Dunkin' Donuts* (they did have cuter outfits back then), *I need to ask around for ideas or a referral.*

So, I did. And someone referred me to their friend at a local employment agency in Schenectady, New York, near where General Electric had one of their corporate office divisions along with thousands of employees, including blue-collar workers; my dad was one of the *blues*.

I had always believed employment agencies were for the corporate elite. But off to the agency I went. I made an appointment based on a friend's referral. The friendly young woman behind the desk sympathized with my tale of woe—losing my cushy job at Yardley of London—and offered to help.

I felt I was slipping to the lowest of lows as I told her how desperate I was. Rent was coming due, and I had no car. I told her I was begging my parents to give me their brown, non-descript '65 Ford Fairlane that had been sitting in the backyard. It was semi-covered with overgrown bushes pushing through the windows and water damaged inside from leaving the windows partly open for months. The car wreaked of a damp odor that permeated the inside of the vehicle and, soon, my clothing.

Musty was never my perfume of choice, especially after being pampered at my dream job with its decent income and pension. I missed spraying delightful fragrances in the air, even if my tongue did swell when doing so. I even got to tweeze and shape women's eyebrows so they could pretend they were Jean Shrimpton or Twiggy while wearing Yardley of London makeup. Those were different times, and sanitary concerns didn't exist. I used my own tweezers. Yikes!

I sadly told my new friend at the employment agency how I had traveled weekly and been treated like a celebrity guest as the Yardley of London representative, working behind some of the best department store counters along the East Coast.

Alas, pride doesn't pay bills.

This nice employment agent flipped through her files, looked up at me, and with a straight face and reassuring smile, asked how I felt about dentists.

"Other than not wanting to date one, they are necessary for health reasons," I replied.

"How would you feel about working with one, being trained as a dental assistant without having to go to a school and getting paid while learning a trade?" she asked.

"Pure white outfits are not my best color," I replied. She informed me I could start the next day, and I didn't have to wear white, not yet anyway, while training. I negotiated the fee and was ready for a new opportunity. I was open.

I showed up in the longest miniskirt I had in the closet. The doctor liked me right away. Of course, it was probably the skirt. No matter, I was in training for a new career with a paycheck!

That day, I learned about patients, paperwork, dentist tools, and setting up for new patients. I even learned how to develop X-ray films. That was fun. The day was humming along, and I was doing okay. At the end of the shift, there was one more patient to go before I could call it a day.

To that point, since I liked meeting the patients, I thought I'd give the job a few weeks to see if it would be a career I could make more permanent while settling down a bit. I'm always open to new possibilities. Besides, rent was due.

The last patient arrived; I made her feel comfortable by smiling while I prepared her in the chair and readied the tools for the doctor. He surprised me by saying I would be assisting him with this patient. He told me to stand in front of her as he prepared her gums for dentures. Okay, I knew family members who had dentures...piece of cake.

As I best remember, he administered Novocain, then shortly after began probing her mouth. Then he grabbed another tool and started extracting teeth. To me, it seemed more like popping corn kernels off a corncob. Pop...pop...pop...and then blood gushed from her jaw. I assumed then I was supposed to assist in cleaning her.

I don't remember much after that, except when I came to, I was splayed out on the floor in my longest miniskirt, hitched up a little higher than I would have wanted, with drool dripping from my mouth.

The cold linoleum felt so good on my face. The doctor looked concerned as he stooped over me, asking if I was okay. I just looked up at him and said, "I don't think this job is for me. Don't worry about paying me. I'm going home now."

The moral of this story—not all opportunities are meant for you. Don't be too open. Instead, trust that the right opportunities will find you. Check in with your heart and check out all referrals. Back in the early '70s, working with people was based on trust and gut feelings. It was not easy. Even though we now have the Internet for fact checking, be forensic in your search.

The next morning, I got a call from the nice agent woman telling me to return to the employment agency, which was required. What now?

The owner wanted to meet me. Oh, joy. Being respectful and not wanting to burn any bridges, I complied and went in to meet with him.

He seemed pretty amused by my story. I was actually embarrassed; however, I laughed when revisiting the events. Someone fainting was a first for their agency. That's me...trendsetter, always leading the way. The scene was a first for me, too, and I scratched dental assistant from my resume.

The agency owner kindly dropped the agency fee, and, to my surprise, offered me a job working for him as an agent. He liked my sense of humor, resume, and people skills. "And don't worry about passing out. I guarantee there will be no blood involved."

I thought, *Sure, why not?* since he was going to train me. This seemed to be a better path than becoming a Dunkin' Donuts Dolly, even if Dunkin'

Donuts did have cuter outfits than McDonald's.

I stayed at the agency for a year, working the sales desk on straight commission and learned a lot about direct sales, people, and body language.

Two important networking tips about body language:

1. When people feel nervous or troubled, they blink more, and it often happens when they are lying or feeling stressed.

2. Always smile as you look someone directly in the eyes, since it breaks down unconscious barriers and puts people at ease. This is helpful in sales *and* dating.

I became pretty good at connecting and matching people, especially women, to appropriate job opportunities. I had to; it was survival, and yet another training ground for learning about connecting people and referrals. I soon gained a following and became a referral source for many women who successfully secured jobs through me. Cha-ching.

While I was successful in meeting quotas and paying my bills, I was still driving that musty old Ford Fairlane. None of my friends would ask me to drive when we went out socially. They complained that their clothes absorbed the odors. I saved a lot of money on gas—not so much on dry cleaning.

However, I soon became restless. And I really needed a new car. I couldn't escape that I had once lived the life of a road warrior in sales, pounding the pavement and enjoying certain freedoms and benefits all while getting paid. I needed a change. This time, I saw an ad in the newspaper, not through the agency. It was for a sales job involving road travel. I knew immediately it had my name on it.

I went for it!

#possibilities

#trusttheuniverse

"Call it a clan, call it a network, call it a tribe, call it a family; whatever you call it, whoever you are, you need one."

— Jane Howard, author

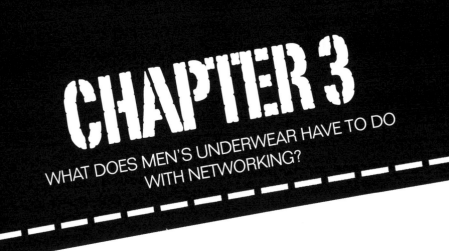

CHAPTER 3

WHAT DOES MEN'S UNDERWEAR HAVE TO DO WITH NETWORKING?

When I interviewed for my next opportunity, it was for a sales position on the road with Hanes. I assumed it was the division that sold pantyhose in those cute little white plastic eggs visible in every supermarket, corner drugstore, and airport. They were hot and hatching everywhere.

We are talking about the mid-seventies when women never left home without pantyhose. They were so popular that even Joe Namath, a quarterback for the New York Jets and cultural icon, wore them in the famous and notably outrageous Beautymist pantyhose commercial in 1974. That's the year I landed the Hanes job and jumped to my all-time high, a low five-figure income including a company car and benefits. That was a hefty monthly paycheck in those days, especially after I was used to the four-figure income I'd had for years.

Yippee! I was on the road again!

The economy was bad, and jobs were scarce, yet I knew I had nailed that two-hour interview with the two corporate suits drilling me about my position with Yardley. They asked me to take a job compatibility test. Later, they revealed they picked me over the 600-plus applicants because I would be doing a similar job to what I was doing with Yardley, and I came with more sales and training experience.

As I was leaving that interview and feeling optimistic, I asked which division I'd be working for since it hadn't come up in any of our conversations.

The division wasn't L'eggs pantyhose; it was the men and boy's underwear division. Yup, men's underwear.

"I can do this," I said. "I have three brothers and a father who wear underwear." Although, they wore Fruit of the Loom because it was more affordable in a family of seven. I would soon learn that Hanes boasts a better fit. Not that I ever wore them.

So, what does men's underwear have to do with networking?

More now than ever, people are looking for a group where they can fit in and truly belong. They want to find a tribe in which they fit perfectly. They seek a no-judgment zone where they can trust and feel trusted sharing life and common interests, one that fosters encouragement, leads, and referrals. Like good underwear, a good fit supports you. I'm stretching this metaphor a bit, but you understand my point.

To find a tribe that fits, you first must do some self reflection to determine what kind of relationships you are seeking. Know thyself. Your inner circle should be a reflection of you and your values.

Be open to new experiences and talk to as many people as possible, everywhere. This is where confidence is essential. More on that later.

Ask around and explore all types of groups to see if the energy feels good on your first visit. Before you commit, go a second time to confirm the good feelings you felt to see if they are still good. This will save money and time by keeping you from jumping in too soon. Organizations you join don't give refunds. I know this all too well.

To grow, you have to be challenged. Ensure the group is inspiring and will lead you in the direction in which you can and want to grow. Push yourself beyond your comfort zone. Leave those comfy slippers at home. They will always be waiting for you when you return.

You'll know your tribe when you find it—at least on the second visit. Like attracts like. Motivational speaker Jim Rohn famously said we are the average of the five people we spend the most time with. To find your tribe, be authentic, kind, and thoughtful.

I strongly believe in being "other-focused" or focused on supporting those you meet. Think about the people you know who need to know the people you meet. Think about which group might be a good fit for a new person you encounter. I believe being other-focused is the key to networking, so it should always be at the top of your mind. Always be connecting. That is not only one of my many secrets, but also good karma.

Suggestions for Finding a Tribe That Matches Your Vibe

The best resource, whether you are a woman or a man, is to go online and search for networks in your local area. Many with specific interests and offerings are available.

I've listed a few organizations for consideration for

fast-tracking your business success.

For Women and Men:

- Local chambers, Rotary, Lions Club, Kiwanis that feature business lunches and dinners—joining one is good, and it's even better to get involved by volunteering on a committee, which will give you visibility and fast-track the process of helping people know you, like you, and trust you. Some chapters may cater to just men or just women or both. Check them out in your area.

- BNI (Business Network International)—World's largest networking group in cities and towns everywhere. Locally, a network may offer a smaller, intimate tribe of both men and women. In this group, only one business type is represented, so you will stand out in your industry. It is based on referrals to the members. Great business connections.

- Meet Ups—these are activity-focused and allow you to network with little to no investment.

- eWomenNetwork—an international women's networking group that accepts a few good men. This group is high-achieving entrepreneurial women supporting a foundation while supporting each other—a favorite of mine.

- Mastermind Groups—bringing people together with a common goal, support, and accountability.

- Women in Business (WIB)—where you work together to achieve personal goals.

Men's and women's groups are everywhere in your surrounding community. Again, seek them out, go to a meeting or two, and see if it feels like your tribe. In this book, you will find some great tools (some of my secret sauce) for engaging when you don't know anyone at these gatherings. Your capital is your relationships!

Gold Nugget Tips:

In every volunteer organization I've been involved in, I quickly rose to a leadership position. I was always the first to volunteer as a greeter when people arrived at check-in. It's a great way to meet everyone quickly and get to know them—and they get to know you.

I also liked to volunteer for phone trees. These are calls to remind people of the upcoming meetings and allow the opportunity to engage in conversation that has nothing to do with selling. This also is a great way to connect with everyone and begin to establish rapport.

While you can reach out to others by sending text messages, I am a diehard phone girl from my early telephone operator days before Yardley.

I am often asked, "Anne, if you could cite just one key to your success, what would it be?" And I *always* give the same answer, "The phone!" Use it.

Still, *nothing* replaces one-to-one, in-person interaction, so do that whenever possible.

To recap the underwear analogy:

Your group, the tribe you are seeking, just like great underwear, needs to be a good fit. If you know the foundation is strong and offers good support that feels right, you will feel secure and comfortable being in it.

Keep reading…we are just getting started.

#greatfit

GOLDEN NUGGET

A top-secret to my success:
The phone—use it! It's the next best
thing to being there.

"Begin with the end in mind."

— Franklin Covey, author

CHAPTER 4
MAKING A LASTING FIRST IMPRESSION: "YOU HAD ME AT HELLO"

Maybe you remember the 1996 movie *Jerry Maguire*, in which Tom Cruise professes his apologetic love to Renée Zellweger by saying, "You complete me." She tearfully responds, "Shut up. You had me at hello." That is one of the most famous movie lines of all time. It left a great impression on viewers. While you may not be professing love to someone you meet, my hope is you will want to make as great a lasting impression as this movie. How will you do that?

"Begin with the end in mind" is Franklin Covey's quote. You have heard at least a thousand times in so many ways, and it's true. In business or in life, you always have a destination, right? Even if you are going to the grocery store, you must set that mental action in motion and then follow through. It's no different for any task or project where you have a *desired* outcome.

Can we talk?

If going to a networking event is one of your destinations, prepare for it in the best possible way. Take it seriously so you don't make just a good first impression but a *great* lasting first impression.

According to Serenity Gibbons, a contributor to *Forbes*, you and your business have seven seconds to make a first impression.[1]

Seven seconds...are you kidding? Saying hello takes one second. Looking someone up and down takes another. Come on; I know you do that first. Everyone does. If you say you don't, you're lying to yourself. It's human nature.

In the next second, you are looking at their face and their eyes and then their smile, and hopefully, they are smiling, and you are too. That's a good start.

Gibbons says, "Seventy-two percent of people say first impressions are impacted by how someone appears and their handshake." Absolutely true. Will handshakes be a thing of the past? I doubt it. What could replace the handshake? Shaking

---

[1] https://www.forbes.com/sites/serenitygibbons/2018/06/19/ you-have-7-seconds-to-make-a-first-impression-heres-how-to-succeed/?sh=69563c656c20. Accessed November 4, 2021.

hands is part of our American culture.

And, yes, of course, how you dress, your grooming, smile, voice, speech, and posture are all in the equation. I will be addressing some of these topics later.

But think about this: Your first impression is your brand. In business today, it seems like everyone is on the "brand wagon" with the how-to and what-to and the best strategies to promote your brand. Whatever your business is, *you* represent your brand. Especially if you are an entrepreneur, *you* are your brand, and there is no one else like you.

Businesses spend thousands of dollars promoting their brand each year. How are you showing up as your brand? How will you make the best first impression in one to seven seconds, convincing a new contact to engage with you?

Every attendee at a networking event has the same goal—growing their business by connecting to their ideal customer, by traveling the journey from not knowing someone to that person becoming their client. How are you distinguishing yourself from a sea of sameness? Or are you there because you know you need to be and you are hiding in some way from being your best or from making a great first impression? Let's explore this more....

We are sending out visual, non-verbal messages all the time. Much can be said about our non-verbal signals, which reflect our personality through our appearance.

I want to share a story from one of my peers, Susan Epstein, who penned this before becoming one of my coaches.

> I was at a live event for 300-plus attendees, all looking to build their coaching businesses with the advice of a well-known coach. I was rooming with a really good friend. She was also my business coach at the time, and she always dressed up, put on her high heels, lipstick, and walked tall.
>
> You know, those hotel conference center rooms are always so cold so the person on the stage isn't sweating. I would usually bring jeans and 400 sweaters and look like a bag lady and sit close to the door. That was so I could use the bathroom every fifteen minutes. I really was hiding because I really didn't want to talk to anybody. After all, I really didn't know who I was yet, and I definitely did not want to join anyone on that stage.
>
> That morning, I said to myself, "I want to be just

like her, my roommate. I want to walk down that wide aisle and go up to the microphone today like everyone else has, strong and confident." I had brought a green dress—just randomly thrown it in my suitcase. It was my best color because I have green eyes. I put on the dress, put on my high heels and lipstick, and when I walked into the elevator and saw a few people I knew, they were like, "Wow," and I was like "Yeah," and I started walking around that room like I owned it.

It wasn't my event, but I noticed that people were starting to come up to me because I was no longer invisible. I was walking around the room with confidence. That day was pivotal for me, and it all started with a green dress.

People *will* judge you according to the way you dress. A 2017 study from Northwestern University revealed that what you wear affects how you think and even perform.[2]

It's still true today, even if we are Zooming more.

What will be your green dress? And if you are a guy reading this, will it be a blue blazer or a white shirt with a tie?

2 https://newyorklifestylesmagazine.com/articles/2017/02/22.html. Accessed November 4, 2021.

Today, apparel has become more relaxed, and business casual has taken on a new meaning. However, if you want to stand out among the sea of sameness, do it with a professional flair.

How will you show up looking confident and strong, reflecting that part of your personality?

Good for you if you already have a handle on this one. You are confident, and you can pass this first impression test with ease. People do business with people they trust. If you show attention to detail in looking put together, they will trust you are like that in your business.

Let's face it: If you *feel* you need help in this area, you probably *do*.

My best tip is to invest time in finding a good fashion consultant or certified stylist like my friends Diane Trone on the Connecticut shoreline and Mary Carangelo in the Hartford area, who can work with your body type and personality. Most stylists will help you go through your closet and put a few outfits together that don't require much thought. This way, you always look fabulous when you are on the run. I think of it as Garanimals, the clothing I used to buy for my kids, the mix-and-match outfits that even the youngest can't mess up.

You can also find stylists in higher-end fashion stores. I have found the most convenient and fun way for women to stay fashionable is to attend shopping parties at the stylists' homes or hosted at a friend's house. They're called trunk shows. At all of the parties I have attended, they serve wine, cheese, and champagne. You don't get that at Nordstrom. I'm optimistic that these parties will remain popular because they are relaxed and fun, with great networking opportunities.

I want to share a cute story about a home party that Diane Trone was having one weekend before she moved her business to a brick-and-mortar showroom.

Diane's Martha Story

Diane was having one of her weekend Trunk Shows at her home where people make appointments and see the latest line of clothing for the season. One of her clients, a lovely ninety-five-year-young fashionista named Martha, called and said she would like to pop over to see the latest line, but she could not commit to the exact time. Diane had to run out to do an important errand, so she asked her husband to let Martha in when she arrived.

When Diane returned from her errand, she walked into her home and, to her surprise, saw Martha wearing Diane's personal clothes, which she had hanging in her hall still in the plastic bag because she had just picked them up from the dry cleaners. Martha had a huge smile on her face, and said, "I love this outfit, Diane. I'll take it! Of course, Diane, laughing, explained to Martha that they were her personal clothes and not for sale. Martha looked sad and told Diane she had a big date that evening and it would be the perfect outfit to wear. Diane could not disappoint an adorable ninety-five-year-young woman who wanted the perfect outfit for her hot date, so she told Martha she was welcome to borrow the clothes and wear them on her date that evening. Go, Martha!

I know Diane, so I know she *will* go above and beyond for her clients!

This one wins the superior customer service award! LOL!

I want to address a small detail that makes a *big* difference, for women especially—accessorize. Jewelry, scarves, shoes...oh, those beautiful shoes. Now that women have gone more casual, will we ever wear heels again? And matching any shoe with the right purse is still just as important for the finishing touches. For both men and women, remember a good hairstyle that fits your face and groomed nails are important. I've seen more men at nail salons where they trim, push back the cuticles, and buff the nails. Nice look. I always say success is in the details.

If you are not sure this relates to you, ask your best friend to tell you the honest truth—at least if you can't trust your mirror.

Fact: Some people are unconsciously conscious about how you are put together, which may be a factor in whether they are attracted to you. This is all non-verbal, of course.

At the end of this book, under Special Reports and Resources, I have listed a few companies I work with, and they all have stylists waiting to help you. I call it Anne's "A List" of VIP Resources. Check it out. I've included some accessories too!

So, what's next?

I want to share the importance of some more non-verbal clues.

Dr. Albert Mehrabian, professor emeritus of psychology at UCLA, has published studies on the relative importance of verbal and nonverbal messages. It's not just our words or tone of voice, but our body language that conveys our true meaning.

He devised a formula to describe how the mind assigns meaning. He concluded that the interpretation of a message is 7 percent verbal (actual words spoken), 38 percent vocal (your tone of voice), and 55 percent visual. Facial and body expressions reflect our emotions and, consequently, our personalities. How a person sees you when you talk, including appearance, facial expressions, and body language (your nonverbal communication), far outweighs the words you are saying.

Why does appearance matter? Nothing is more effective than *in-person* interactions. That is why I am personally a *huge* fan of face-to-face connecting, and if you can't do it face-to-face, Zoom is a close second.

In addition to appearances, active listening is also key to making a strong first impression and effectively networking.

Here are a few critical tips for showing you are actually *listening* and interested in the person you are with:

- Smile and look directly into their eyes to make them feel like they are the only person in the room.

- Your posture should be leaning in with interest, with your upper body directly in front of them, showing an open heart. Note that a person moves closer to the things they like and moves away from something they don't. I am not referring to bad breath. I mean unconscious, non-verbal clues.

- Focus on the person you are with. If you look around the room while in conversation, it will seem as though they aren't important enough to hold your interest. Besides, it's rude.

- How attentive are you? Nodding your head up and down and smiling will acknowledge that you are listening to what they are saying. If you are shaking your head left to right, it will show you disagree with them. People do this unknowingly and send unconscious messages.

- Keep your stance solid and confident. It shows you are grounded.

- Moving your body and using hand gestures will show your excitement and interest.

- Give full attention by turning off your phone. When in a conversation, don't even look at it if it buzzes. If you look at your phone, it says whoever you are speaking with is not as important as whoever is calling. Remember, you are building trust. This is business time. Treat this like an interview. The only possible exception would be to inform the person you are waiting for a possible emergency call from a family member...otherwise, ignore your phone.

- Did you know most hiring decisions are made in the first ten seconds of a job interview? That says volumes, so when networking and meeting a potential client, think of it as an interview in which you really want the job and make a great first impression.

- A practice tip: Stand in front of a mirror. Have a conversation with the person on the other side as if you were meeting them for the first time. Really? Yes, really. If this is weird to you, okay, it's weird. Practice with a friend and ask for feedback. Do it—practice makes perfect.

Consider using these tips to help make a great and lasting first impression.

Good luck. You've got this.

#greatlastingfirstimpression

Golden Nugget

Focus on the person you meet.
Make them feel as though they
are the most important person
in the world, because at that
moment, they are.

"Efforts and courage are not enough without purpose and direction."

— President John F. Kennedy

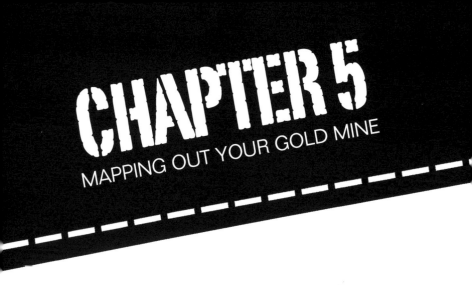

CHAPTER 5
MAPPING OUT YOUR GOLD MINE

There's gold in them hills!

Let's say it's 1848, and like many other Gold Rushers, you are setting out to seek your fortune by searching for gold in the California hills.

Before you can head out in search of gold, you need to know where California is on a map (if there were any in 1848) or just head west and follow the trail of others. You also want to get prepared for the trip.

It will take a lot of courage, purpose, and direction—planning will be necessary.

Let's shift gears.

I propose you think of networking as if you preparing to join the gold rush and seek your fortune and a better life—meeting a potential client is your gold.

And *why* are you traveling to a place you have never been with people you don't know? Oh right, risk and

reward. You are seeking a fortune in gold, for prosperity and a better life. Gold is money. Money is
power. Shh. That's just like networking.

Plan ahead, make a list:

- ☐ Know your purpose and your why. What is
  your goal?

- ☐ Plan your strategy and direction.

- ☐ Prepare for problems.

Like most people, your goals for business growth
opportunities probably cover many areas. Here
are a few:

- ☐ New clients and connections

- ☐ New ideas

- ☐ Promotion of products or services

- ☐ Community and support

- ☐ Making the cash register ring

Let's address each one listed above:

Do you want new clients and connections? That is
what everyone in business wants. Networking at
events can give you a wider reach and more exposure. Networking helps generate opportunities

for referrals and finding jobs. It also helps in establishing connections for business collaboration. Networking is your Net Worth!

Networking is an opportunity to gain knowledge and new ideas. It's a great way to learn about people and businesses different from yours. It gives you more depth and exposure to more people, places, and ideas to help *you* grow.

Are you networking to promote your products or services? You have the opportunity to share new products and new services, promotions, or your new book in a variety of ways. Without being salesy, you can be a vendor, sponsor, or speaker.

Community and support: Networking offers a great opportunity to build lifelong friendships with people who share your interests. Maybe you need help in a specific area of your business. Everyone has a list of top resources in their circle, and they are usually willing to share them once you establish trust.

Making the cash register ring: You really can do business networking if you do it right and do not scare people away with a used car sales approach. It's serving, not selling.

Plan Your Strategy

Let's assume you are going to go mine a cave. Once you arrive at your desired destination, how are you going to find the gold? Are you going to start randomly swinging a pickaxe, or do you have a strategy? In Chapter 8: Mining for Gold, I write about how to work a room—who to approach and why.

How will you manage to extract the gold when you think you have found it? I address this in Chapter 9: Digging in the Mine—Going Deeper, where I discuss how to ask engaging questions.

Just like in networking, you always need a strategy and a plan to connect and find more gold…I mean, attract more clients.

Prepare for Problems

Sometimes, you have a bad day in the mines, or you realize that just because everyone else is shoulder-to-shoulder and finding some success, that doesn't mean it's the right place for you. Maybe it's not the right mine, so you need to look for another space and tribe.

Maybe you are in the right place, but you met some super-obnoxious person who turns you off. How do you move on gracefully? This is one of my best secrets, and I address this situation in Chapter 8.

Next up: Selling *you*—twelve tips you may find helpful.

#planyourstrategy

#prepareforproblems

"Let the light of your presence illuminate
every room you enter."

— Wayne Gerard Trotman, British
independent filmmaker

CHAPTER 6
SELLING YOURSELF IS AN ART

Networking Magic: Twelve Tips for Making People Love You Immediately

When you are serious about selling yourself in a competitive field, having talent and being clever are essential. However, nothing replaces *a charismatic personality* or, as I will refer to it in this book, ACP.

#acharismaticpersonality

Lloyd Price released a song back in 1959 called "Personality." I know I am really dating myself here; however, I heard that song as the youngest of five with four much older siblings. I was impressionable and forced to watch Dick Clark on a black-and-white TV after school when I preferred the Mouseketeers.

In the song, Price tells his love they have personality, they walk with it, talk with it, etc. I now believe hearing that song over and over set me on an early course of self-affirmations, which led to self-confidence and, ultimately, success.

Gaining insight into how you make someone love you immediately starts with a positive attitude. Looking straight into someone's eyes, while smiling, offering a firm handshake, and continuing with a warm opening question, will begin the actual conversation and connection.

I read Dale Carnegie's book *How to Win Friends and Influence People* when I was a gawky, freckle-faced redhead of thirteen. I thought I needed a lifeline and fast. I was not the prettiest girl in school. Actually, I thought I looked more like *Mad Magazine*'s Alfred E. Newman's little sister, although I was a bit of a flirt and personable. I certainly stood out as one of two redheads in the entire school. However, I believe it was my fun-loving, upbeat personality that got me noticed.

Upon reflection, I am hands-down certain that ACP (a charismatic personality) was my ticket into sales and marketing right out of high school, even though I had no experience. The rest was up to me. I had to be resourceful and work hard to be successful, although I did stumble a bit.

Over the years, I have identified the most intriguing tips I have successfully used when networking. They will work, whether you are shy or outgoing, and help you build your ACP muscle while adding points to your ACP value.

How charismatic are you?

Being charismatic is not about being an extrovert or an introvert.

Take the ACP quiz in the Special Reports and Resources section or see the link there to download it from my website. Find out how your charismatic personality rates and learn some tips to help improve it.

#acharismaticpersonality

Read on for more networking magic.

Here are twelve tips that have worked for me. Some may be new to you, and some you may have used before. I encourage you to try them, even old ones you may not have used in a while. They say everything old becomes new again.

Tip 1: Building Rapport, Match and Mirror

One of my favorite tools for building rapport, one I learned from the Anthony (Tony) Robbins Institute, is "Match & Mirror." Here's a story of how I used it:

Do you know that *like* attracts *like*? I have met women, and we fell "in like" immediately, such as with my West Coast friend Deborah Stuart, founder and CEO of High Chi Energy Jewelry (see the "A List" of VIP Resources in Special Reports and Resources section). I swear, when we first met at an eWomen networking event in Dallas, we knew we must be sisters from another mister. We bonded at once.

Why is that?

Then there are the times when you meet someone and they seem interesting, yet there is something you can't quite put your finger on, so you step back a little. Although now that I am older and wiser, I say give everyone a chance. You can't love everything about everyone. However, you can find a common interest to advance your connection. It's a business, not a marriage.

And as you will read many times in this book, you never know who they know who may need to know you.

Attending Tony Robbins Institute taught me about building rapport. Tony says, "Rapport is power!" What is rapport? Rapport is the total responsiveness between people. When you respond to someone, and they respond to you, you are in rapport and communion. There is that connection, that spark that happens in particular communications and relationships.

That is what happened when I first met Deborah, a spark and immediate connection. Our sensory acuity was the same, facial and physical expressions the same. We even looked like we could be sisters. Our tone of voice and tempo was the same. It's a beautiful thing when that instant connection happens. Since meeting a few years ago, we have helped each other in business with referrals. Our rapport was built with trust and is ongoing.

People like people who are like themselves, or who are like how they would like to be. People pull back from people who are not like themselves or who don't represent what they want to be—it is sad but true.

Some of you may remember playing "monkey see, monkey do" as a kid and mimicking everything the other person was doing. It would sometimes make you a little crazy. Match and mirror isn't quite like our kids' game; replicating other people's movements would be weird as an adult. Although matching the person's voice tempo, fast or slow, would be a type of match and mirror. You can match the volume, soft or loud, or the tone of voice. Also, you could subtly mirror hand gestures and facial expressions with your mouth and eyes. You would be surprised by how well you connect with someone when doing so.

An excellent exercise would be to observe in a live networking group to see if you can see mirroring happening. Also, give it a go to see how it works for you. It really does work.

#buildrapport

#matchandmirror

Tip 2: The Cut-and-Run

Has this ever happened to you? You are at a networking meeting, someone approaches you to connect, and you sense immediately you have nothing in common. Before you dash off, remember, it's important not to cut and run after a minute of talking to someone just because they don't seem to fit the profile of the perfect client. Be aware that they may know many people you don't know, and they may just know someone who needs to know you. It could end up being a good referral, but if you cut and run, you may never know. I have seen this happen hundreds of times. I touched on this in Chapter 1.

After decades of connecting with people, I have come to believe every person is born with a special gift unique to them. For some, it reveals itself early in life; for others, it's later—they are late bloomers.

When you meet someone, if you choose to take the time and effort to stop and listen, you may discover they have a special message for you to hear. In the end, any chance meeting or coincidence may be serendipity.

Here is a story about an experience I had as a young girl. It changed my perspective on people.

The Gift

One morning when I was in fifth grade, I arrived at elementary school to see a beautifully wrapped gift on the teacher's desk.

The box held our English assignment for the coming week. It was to be our initiation into public speaking. We were all told we would write a speech and deliver it at the end of the week. Each topic was written on a piece of paper and waiting for us to pull from the gift box. The speech needed a beginning, middle, and end. And we needed an interesting opening.

When it was my turn, I reached my little hand into the gift box with eager anticipation. I pulled out the paper, opened it up, and stared at it dumbfounded.

The paper read, "a piece of glass." I asked my best friend, Debbie, what she got.

"A dress," she replied happily.

"Trade ya," I said.

"No deal," said Debbie. Her mom was a dress-maker.

What was I going to say about a piece of glass?

That evening, I was washing dishes. While staring at a clear juice glass for inspiration, it slipped from my small, soapy hand and smashed on the counter. As I picked up the largest shard and held it up, the setting sun shone through the window and caught the ragged edge of the glass. A prism shined back at me and onto the wall.

That got me thinking: Something I thought was useless was really beautiful if seen in the right light. I kept that broken piece of glass, and my speech was born. I worked on the speech all week.

When the day came to deliver my speech, I was excited to share my interesting opening—I held a clear drinking glass in my hand, wrapped it with a cloth napkin, then pulled a tall metal garbage pail toward me, and with all of my might, I thrust the glass in the pail, expecting it to break.

It bounced.

My classmates giggled.

Embarrassed, I quickly reached into the pail, grabbed the glass, and thrust it again to smash it. It bounced again. By this time, kids were roaring with laughter. And me? I was so overcome with embarrassment that I was sweating. My face was red as a tomato, and I was in emotional pain. Honestly, I don't remember what happened after that.

If the glass had shattered and I could have shown a piece of glass with its ragged edges, I would have told my classmates that it reminded me of the many facets of people and how each person is unique even with their ragged edges. If given the opportunity to be seen in the right light, with the edges reflecting as a prism, people are beautiful and not to be discarded no matter how different or ugly. I was way ahead of my time.

Six-plus decades later, as I reflect on that unpleasant memory and all the people I have met and connected with, I still look for the gift in each person I meet.

G – is the *greatness* we all possess. We come into this world to learn what we are to teach.

I – is for *influence* and *inspiration*—go out and

share your big message; the world needs to hear it.

F – is for *focus*—find your tribe and market to that niche. Go narrow and deep.

T – is for *truth*—be transparent and vulnerable and trust yourself.

When meeting with a new person, no matter how different they may seem, take the time to ask questions to find a commonality of interest. Look for the GIFT. At the very least, leave the conversation feeling fulfilled on some level. Even though it may not be an ideal client fit, it is a connection. A warm contact outranks a cold call any day of the week.

#GIFT

#nocutandrun

#nocoldcall

Tip 3: Expressing Positive Energy

Have you been at a meeting when someone walks into the room and radiates light and energy? You can just tell they are a people magnet. That's magic.

The energy you project can determine the success of your connections. Here is where that big, sincere smile is so important. With that sparkle in your eyes, and obviously just being happy in the moment, you can usually grab almost anyone's attention. Who doesn't want to be around that person?

What if you are the quieter type and not a flash of bright light entering the room?

That is when you can communicate, with a warm smile on your face and in your eyes, a genuine interest in the person you are meeting. That is the starting point in expressing positive emotions and energy. People are affected by other people's moods, so when you are with someone, focus on positive thoughts and gratitude and you will exude positive energy. A positive mindset can make a big difference in communication.

I am a big believer in affirmations. I recite several, starting my morning with gratitude sessions every day and often throughout the day. Consider reciting the following affirmations or others you find inspiring before you go into a networking event—when in the car or while walking into the building. They will put you in a positive state.

- "When I look for the good in everything, I attract it to myself."

- "Positive thoughts bring me benefits and advantages I desire."

- "Every day, in every way, I am getting better and better."

You can always substitute "better" for "stronger," "healthier," "happier," or whatever you want to focus on that day. It works.

When you make others feel happy by being around you and you communicate positive emotions, you will benefit and score more ACP points in the most positive way.

Caution: I love honesty. However, if you are not feeling your best or suffering somehow, stay home and call a friend you can dump it on. Never talk about your problems, worries, diseases, or illnesses at a networking gathering. The more negative energy you give off, the worse your connections will be. It is better to make no impression at all than a bad one. TMI (too much information) is usually a turn-off when it comes to life's woes. You will be perceived as a whiner and not a winner.

Remember: Always be positive in thought and word— it will score you ACP points and attract business.

#bepositivebehappy

Tip 4: Be a Good Listener (bears repeating)

Listening should be a given at any networking event. As I said in Chapter 4, and will emphasize more throughout this book, I usually start by asking questions and encouraging others to talk about themselves and their businesses, showing a sincere interest in them.

To become a good conversationalist is to become a good listener. To be a good listener, you must care, really listen, and focus on what people have to say. There is a big difference between listening to and hearing someone. Sometimes people don't want an entertaining conversation partner. They just want someone who will listen to them. Doing so is being kind. And it scores high marks in achieving a charismatic personality (ACP).

#listenmoretalkless

Tip 5: Be Caring, Kind, and Nice

Let's clarify caring, kind, and nice. Fine lines exist between being caring, kind, and nice.

Being nice is being polite; being kind is caring and showing genuine interest in others. Nice is inauthentic—and who could trust *that*?

We all know people who can play nice in the business sandbox because it is appropriate, yet they may be unkind as soon as they leave. Conversely, someone can care about you and still mistreat you. Many, women especially, identify this as emotional abuse. I have had first-hand experience. I've been there.

One famous example is the movie or Broadway show *My Fair Lady*. It has a great message about the difference between kindness and being nice.

The story unfolds as the kind and caring Eliza Doolittle, a common flower girl found on the streets of London, is transformed into a refined, well-spoken lady. The phonetics professor, Henry Higgins, tells his colleague, Colonel Pickering, that he could pass her off as a duchess.

Henry Higgins believes that language is the barrier between the upper and lower classes. In the end, after Eliza's transformation, she leaves Henry Higgins, despite caring deeply for him. She says he is polite and nice, yet consistently unkind, mistreating and disparaging her for being the common flower girl she once was. In contrast, Colonel Pickering is kind and caring, treating her well during her transformation as a duchess. His attitude toward Eliza has nothing to do with class level.

What does this have to do with business and networking? Today, especially, I believe we need to show more kindness to all people. We live in a world full of snap judgments based on first impressions, and people are not always kind. This poor judgment could backfire in business.

Remember, sincere smiles, attentive listening, and genuine caring for the people you meet make your ACP score soar higher.

#bekind

#becaring

Tip 6: Your Nametag

When attending a meeting, if you are handed a nametag, *always* wear it on the right side and above a pocket if you have one. The theory is, when you shake someone's hand, their eyes go to your nametag because most people shake right-handed. I can always tell a rookie networker when their nametag is on the left side. I believe your eyes should bypass the nametag, and you should look them in the eyes first and smile, but we all peek. It's also great to say their name as you shake hands. ("Hello, Sarah James. Nice to meet you.") As you shake their hand, imprint a unique feature that stands out about them in your brain so you can associate that with their name when you reconnect. It may be beautiful hair, nice dimples, or jewelry you admired, etc.

Remembering and acknowledging someone later will definitely score ACP points.

#rememberfeatures

Tip 7: Ask Better Questions (everyone gets hung up on this one)

I am often asked how to approach someone you don't know at networking meetings. Here is what *not* to do....

The hairs on the back of my neck stand up when someone, usually a man, asks me the typical networking question, "What do you do?" To me, it is like nails scratching on a chalkboard. Please avoid this question when meeting someone for the first time. It is icky. It feels like speed networking, and if the person doesn't think you have anything to offer their business, they quickly dismiss you and move on to the next person.

Whoa! Have you ever felt that way at a networking event? I want you to know there is a better approach.

More than likely, you are wearing a nametag, and it may have your company name listed. I love my company name on my nametag not because I am a narcissist, but because it's vague and non-descriptive. It invites people to ask me questions. What is Anne Garland Enterprises? Yes, the two of us are off to a good start.

If I haven't led the conversation by asking a provoking question first, I am usually asked: "What is Anne Garland Enterprises?" I then drop one of my provocative one-sentence intros and turn it around with a question to them. I have plenty of time to talk about me—I want to know with whom I have come face to face.

The key is to find something in common so you can begin to build rapport. Make sure you keep their best interest at heart. It's a trust builder. I address this in detail in Chapter 9: Digging in the Mine—Going Deeper.

#askbetterquestions

Tip 8: Complimenting and Acknowledging Others

Let's clarify how to compliment and acknowledge.

Compliments can be perceived as artificial brown-nosing if they are not sincere. However, acknowledging someone's value and accomplishments shows more understanding of the person, which could rev up your ACP score.

Genuinely praising others without being sappy is incredibly positive. It is a great way to meet someone you have wanted to meet. Maybe you read that they recently received an award or nomination, were published, etc. Acknowledging success is a top ice breaker; it allows you to listen and show interest in others.

People love to talk about their latest successes. Why not be supportive and praise the good? Just remember to be sincere.

Another great approach is saying you heard the buzz on the street about their excellent service, product, staff, or whatever *if it is true.*

Be careful when using the "I" word in giving any compliment, i.e., "I love that dress." However, women accept compliments more easily than men, especially if we are talking about shoes. What woman doesn't love shoes?

The bottom line is that acknowledging someone's value shows you are interested and have noticed them. This practice leads to higher ACP points.

One time at a networking meeting, I had just heard about a new restaurant that was the talk of the town. I had not been there yet, but I knew it was getting rave reviews in all categories. The owner was at the event. I had never met him. I am always seeking new places to hold my women's events, so I took this great opportunity to approach him and tell him about the buzz on the street. He was beaming. Then I asked if the restaurant accommodated larger events. It turned out to be a good connection. I booked it for an event, and it was a hit with my ladies. A perfect win-win for all of us. Great marketing for him.

#complimentwisely

Tip 9: Embracing Vulnerability as an Asset, Shy or Not

Vulnerability is not a weakness; it's authentic. Be yourself. It takes courage to be vulnerable and transparent, to be *you* in the world, warts and all, showing your human side.

"When we dare to drop the armor that protects us from feeling vulnerable, we open ourselves to the experiences that bring purpose and meaning to our lives."

— Dr. Brené Brown, author of *The Power of Vulnerability*

In *The Power of Vulnerability*, Dr. Brené Brown dispels the cultural myth that vulnerability is risky and a sign of weakness. She reveals that it is, in truth, our most accurate measure of courage.

I believe what Brown says. It is okay to be vulnerable, and I know why most shy people don't like networking. Their vulnerability may surface, and it's terrifying. Guess what…we all have stories, some not so pretty, but those stories are our foundation and the building blocks to success.

So, here's my deal: I can get emotional in a New York-minute. I am genuinely open to the emotions I feel even when I don't want to show them, but I do show them. One of my best gal pals loves to make me tear up at the close of my events. As strong a person as I am, it shows I am honest, and I care. I care about people, especially women, and their lives.

I want to help them, which is why I am writing this book.

Networking is effortless to me now because it is a muscle I had to develop early. Being the youngest of five, I wanted to be noticed. I knew I was loved, but I was always the last on the family list. Both parents had to work, and since my older siblings were busy, I was alone a lot. It's probably why I like being social. My maiden name starts with a W, so growing up, I was always last in lines in school. It's no wonder I want to be first whenever possible.

What does this have to do with networking? Be yourself. As Oscar Wilde said, "Be yourself. Everyone else is already taken." That is one of my favorite quotes.

Don't worry about keeping a stiff upper lip—get real, which leads me to my next tip.

#nostiffupperlip

Tip 10: Having a Sense of Humor

Humor is an underused tool that, when adequately infused in your stories, will lift up any conversation. Humor puts others at ease. People want to work with people they like. According to Dale Carnegie, using humor in conversation is a great way to win friends and influence people. I totally agree. I believe that in each industry, no matter how dry, we can find funny stories to share.

GOLDEN NUGGET

Keep a small notebook and note any amusing stories that happen in your day that you can share in a future conversation when appropriate.

#bizarretalesfromthejourney

I got this idea of keeping a small notebook from my comedian friend, Elaine Williams. I met her at a networking event and always enjoy her energy and stories. The following story is one that made her stand out in my mind and made me want to add her to speed dial.

Elaine's Story:

> I was still "new" at networking and feeling very un-comfortable in my own skin. I used to drink for liq-uid courage, so doing daytime networking around women was a triple whammy for me. I found my-self next to a woman in the buffet line whose back-ground, like mine, had been in the theatre. We started discussing how we incorporated all that we'd learned as performers into our businesses.
>
> I could tell she'd been a real player in her other life, and as I listened to her experience, I began to feel even more anxious. I found myself wanting to impress her or at least prove that I had done some cool stuff too.
>
> Mind you, she was not really gloating, but my inse-curities were raging.
>
> I started talking about some singing I'd done and said, "Oh yes, when I was in Austin, Texas, I did some Acapulco singing."
>
> Acapulco!
>
> I'd meant to say "a capella," which means singing without any instruments accompanying you. But instead, I'd said Acapulco, which is a place in Mex-ico. A very different meaning.

She looked confused. I was horrified at my mistake, which I realized immediately. It became even more awkward. Then I blushed, laughed, and made fun of myself. Inside, I was dying.

Somehow, I got through the buffet without embarrassing myself further and promptly found a seat far, far away from her.

Nerves will cause you to do and say stupid things sometimes.

Thank God I kept practicing getting over my social anxiety.

As Elaine shared this story, she said, "Now, if you'll excuse me, I must go practice my escalator pitch…."

What a great punch line. That's Elaine!

Here's another story—one of the most outrageous stories I have heard at a networking dinner. Needless to say, we became the loudest table at the event. To this day, I question its veracity, but the man who told it swears it's true—so bizarre.

Steve and I became friendly at a monthly chamber event. I learned his family owned a department store, and when not working there, he had a side gig as a part-time funeral director. Those who know me know

I can ask some interesting questions, and he was a willing target. He was quite the storyteller and often shared a few stories he made funny by taking the emotion out of a tragedy or serious situation. This technique reminded me of the popular HBO series *Six Feet Under*, which helped people look at death differently. I'm partial to *Six Feet Under* because my daughter, Lauren Ambrose, played Claire Fischer, a lead role on the show, and won several Emmys. That's going back a few years; however, this story could have been one of their weekly segments, it's that bizarre.

Steve's story:

Grandma Goes Snowmobiling

A mother, father, their two children, and grandma go on a winter vacation to the northeast snow country. They hitch a trailer carrying two snowmobiles to the car.

On the way, grandma dies. Unfortunately, they are in the middle of nowhere, no cell phones back then, no nearby houses or hospitals. They are way north on back roads, and they can't leave her dead in the backseat with the kids. To the horror of the wife, since it was her mother, the husband wraps and covers grandma and then straps her to one of the snowmobiles to keep her cold so the body doesn't decompose before getting to their destination.

After traveling on deserted roads for a while and approaching their destination, the kids needed a rest stop and food. They reached a small restaurant and ate quickly. At this point, they don't want to tell anyone grandma is outside riding shotgun in the cold on one of their snowmobiles.

They return to the car and, to their horror and panic, discover someone had stolen the trailer with the snowmobiles!

Of course, I had a hundred questions. I don't remember much more after that, but I never forgot this story or Steve telling it. He swore it was true.

I have sometimes asked someone to share the funniest story relating to their industry or business. It can be an excellent icebreaker for certain.

Death is not a typical topic that comes up as humor, and I apologize if I have offended you.

If you have a funny story about anything in your daily or client interactions, send it to me at anneg@annegarlandenterprises.com—I will notify you if I post it on my website. Please do not share real names and let me know if I can post your name, city, and state.

In the subject line write: Unusual Networking Story

I never met a person who didn't like to laugh. Sure, life circumstances get in the way, and we all have tough days—that's life, but laugh more. It's good for you.

#funnystories

#bizarrestories

#laughmore

Tip 11: Connect and Be a Matchmaker

Some of the most gratifying networking meetings I have attended have been ones in which I met one person and then met someone else, saw a match, and connected them right there at the event because they had what each other needed.

This goes back to, *"Who do you know who needs to know you?"*

This is being an *influencer.*

An associate of mine invited me to an invitation-only networking meeting in a different part of the state. The format was informal networking for two hours, depending on your arrival time. We feasted on pre-dinner hors d'oeuvres, and then enjoyed a sit-down dinner with no assigned seating. We could sit with anyone or choose at random. I chose randomly so I could meet people I hadn't met already. Dessert and coffee were served, and then we went home. No speeches or introductions—everyone was on their own to make their own magic. I loved this event. I had more fun going around meeting both men and women, and, yes, there was a lot of "What do you do?" flying around. Ugh. What I loved about meeting so many people was the opportunity to meet one person and connect and then meet another, and then discover that the two should click because they have what each other needs. I made the introduction right there on the spot. Bam!

This is an extreme example of a networking meeting where I made some solid contacts by connecting other people.

#beamatchmaker

Tip 12: The Two Most Important Words

Here is one more valuable, important tip to add to your list. I have practiced this for years, and it's straight out of Dale Carnegie's book, with my interpretation.

When I ask this question in a group workshop, "What

are the two most important words to any person?" I get all kinds of answers like love, trust, honesty, etc. Those are critical values for certain. However, the two most important words to any person are their first and last names. Say it wrong, spell it wrong, address it wrong, and it will be corrected—sometimes with fury.

I remember a problem at the registration desk at one of my women's empowerment conferences. At these conferences, I personally oversee nametags and work hard to ensure the correct spelling of all of the guests' names. I know how important a person's name and title are. In this instance, "Dr." was missing from a physician's nametag. She was enraged, and just handwriting "Dr." would not do for her.

I got called over and had to intervene. I thought, *Really*? I've got twenty-six speakers, 150 people here moving in all directions, and this was her hot issue. This was a rare exception, of course. However, it really highlighted for me the value of a name.

The point is:

> "Remember that a person's name is, to that person, the sweetest and most important sound in any language."
>
> — Dale Carnegie

Your name is what your individual identity is built around. So be mindful when you meet someone for the first time. Clearly repeat the person's name correctly and interject it appropriately into the conversation so you will remember it in the future.

Also, when at a restaurant, take the time to ask the server for their name and treat them with respect when dining. It makes your dining experience so much more enjoyable.

It doesn't matter if you are a high-energy personality, a nurturer, knowledge/scientist type, CPA, lawyer, or politician. We all deal with the public and want to be liked and respected in our area of expertise.

By being aware of what can help build your *charismatic personality* muscle, you can confidently engage with anyone anywhere. Take the quiz!

Of all the tips I shared, which tip resonated most with you? Ask a good friend to work with you to practice some of the tips in this chapter. Have fun in the process. I would love to get feedback about which one worked best for you…and yet there is so much more to come.

Onward and upward.

#yournamematters

GOLDEN NUGGET

Pick your favorite tip and make it your own.

"There is so much we can do to render service,
to make a difference in the world—no matter how
large or small our circle of influence."

— Stephen Covey, author

CHAPTER 7
EXPAND YOUR CIRCLE OF INFLUENCE

Until I was eighteen, I lived on a beautiful lake in upstate New York. I was mesmerized in the early mornings when the lake was serenely still and smooth as glass. It was the best time of day to sit on our dock and reflect; little did I know my soul was teaching me meditation at an early age.

I enjoyed skimming small, flat rocks across the smooth water and seeing how many times it would skip. When I missed the skim, it would plunge and ripple—first small circular waves, then bigger circles that would stretch out farther and farther. I was fascinated by the distance those little ripples spread. Depending on how fast the rocks skipped or plunged, many waves would cross over each other and keep rippling as they overlapped.

I find networking similar to the cause-and-effect ripples of that lake. It's like I am the rock plunging into the networking waters, creating concentric circles of overlapping people and personalities. The ripples are the connections

I have made and influenced outwardly.

The word influencer is tossed around a lot in networking and social media circles. What and who is an "Influencer?"

Influencer: noun, a person or group that can influence the behavior or opinions of others.[3]

Influencers:

- Are people with loyal followers who trust them.
- Are people who attract the right people to a brand.
- Vary depending on the brand segment, which is how a company markets to a certain group and a customer responds to a brand, including their purchasing and spending habits.
- Are trusted and credible in their recommendations.
- Can make a lot of money on social media platforms.
- Dedicate the time needed to become influential.
- Have a minimum of 5,000 followers to become an influencer.

Influencers can be many top-rated TV or movie personalities. Then there are top sports figures. All are paid for endorsements, but are they trusted?

3 Cambridge Advanced Learner's Dictionary & Thesaurus © Cambridge University Press

It's a new world out there where everyone wonders whom they can trust. Interestingly, we tend to trust our peers most for recommendations on movies, restaurants, travel, etc. That is why referrals are so important.

However, some regular people who have caught the eyes of others on social media platforms are now top influencers because they are transparent, showcase a unique flair in some areas, and boast mega-lists of loyal followers. And they get paid well.

If you are not a paid social media icon, you can still make a difference on a smaller scale locally. If you are really interested in being an influencer, you can find many online courses and coaches to get you started.

Below, I've listed six strengths that most influencers have in common.

1. Are trustworthy, consistent, and reliable.

I love this metaphor from Jeff Boss, the adaptability coach: "Building trust is fundamental to increasing your circle of influence. Be consistent because once you break that trust, it's like taking a piece of paper, wrinkling it up, and then trying to flatten it out again—it never actually returns to its original state."

Well said.

Being consistent and dependable will allow you to develop long-term professional relationships and win jobs and trust.

Spend more time doing what you talk about and not talking about what you do.

2. **Make time for people, aka community management.**

    Not only do you have to cultivate a following, but you must interact with your community consistently, answering questions while engaging them. You must know their interests and be sensitive to their needs.

    Like the Beatles, I have often said, "The love you make is equal to the love you take." In other words, *Make time for people and they will make time for you.* I love that!

    Loyal followers are listening—and you are influencing.

3. **Continue to learn and grow. Be authentic.**

    Personal development is critical for influential reach. Grow the best you, and others will trust and follow you as long as you remain authentic.

4. Are non-judgmental.

Have your opinions, yet keep an open mind and be more accepting of others; then you will attract more opportunities and friends. Inviting negativity into your life is not a good reflection of you.

5. Are experts at creating content.

Focus on your one thing that makes you stand out by being creative and inspiring to capture competing attention. I see so many copycats lip-syncing the same songs. Be original and you will succeed.

People are talking about influencer marketing. What is it?

According to Wikipedia, influencer marketing is a form of social media marketing involving endorsements and product placement from influencers, people, and organizations who have a purported expert level of knowledge or social influence in their field.

Purchasing decisions have changed over the years with more online opportunities, thus giving rise to influencer marketing. Many big brands use influencer marketing to reach their target audiences through many media platforms. Smaller businesses are using influencers in a variety of social media platforms too.

Good luck. You've got this!

#beaninfluencer

Golden Nugget

My Five Tips to Becoming an Influencer

1. Be an expert. Find your niche.

2. Know your audience's interests.

3. Be visible on LinkedIn/Twitter/Facebook. Connections are everything.

4. Develop your content strategy. Be creative.

5. Distribute your content consistently.
   Does this sound like you? Ready to give it a go?

"A simple hello could lead to a million things."

— Nicola Jones-Crossley, writer,
researcher, business consultant

CHAPTER 8
MINING FOR GOLD

D o you know whom to approach at a networking meeting and how to approach them?

Here is a brief note from a happy networking convert:

I've always known the importance of relationships in business and that networking is a great way to develop those relationships. But I would overwhelm myself trying to network with as many people as possible because I thought that was what I was supposed to do. This left me feeling frustrated. When I heard Anne Garland speak at a women's event, she changed everything for me. She shared her 3-2-1 method, a tool for Networking. Talk about an "aha" moment! Since that time, using this tool has helped me make significant and lasting connections. It has removed decision fatigue around "Who should I meet?" "Did I meet 'enough' people?" "What should I say?" In other words, I'm not worried about doing it right because I'm using a tool that shows me how. Thank you, Anne!

— Kathy Keegan, ACC, CPC, ELI-MP, New York City, 2019

Thank *you*, Kathy Keegan!

Have you often wanted to know how to work a room? Folks, my 3-2-1 method is worth a million dollars or at least the price of this book.

Now *you* can experience a surefire way to overcome a lack of confidence or shyness while working the room. I call it my 3-2-1 method, aka "Split Second Connection."

If you have read this far, hopefully by now you realize the benefits of networking. Now let's get to work!

Seize the Day

Your calendar says this is the day; it will be an essential gathering....

You are looking your best, ready to make an impression and make some connections.

Let's go!

You arrive, look for a familiar face in the crowd, and

see *no one you know. Yikes!* Now what?

This is when you start doubting yourself and begin the negative self-talk. You say things like, "Why am I here? I don't know anyone. I hate these events." Sound familiar? You continue to scan the room for a recognizable face…please, dear God, someone I know, please show up. Not happening…what do you do?

You have options:

- Stall and go to the restroom, waiting for someone you might know to show up. The bathroom is wonderful for taking a breather and not having to talk to anyone.

- Head to the buffet and start eating. After all, you paid for this event and should get your money's worth.

- Exit, head home, and waste a great opportunity to meet someone you could help with your business, may have a connection for you, or could benefit from knowing you and become a significant lead.

Or

You could try out my never-fail Split Second Connection method of introducing yourself to a few people you have never met before.

What the heck—you have invested money to attend the event, driving time, and parking fees. You've given up additional time from your already packed schedule, or worse, maybe even paid for a babysitter. Better yet, you just bought this great pair of shoes, and you know you look *hot*.

This investment may have cost you close to $100 plus the cost of the fantastic shoes.

You've decided you are going for it. You're going in. Bravo!

Here is how it works.

You scan the room and look for someone you would like to meet. Someone who has a kind face and is standing or sitting by themselves is a good find. This is Key #1 *and* very important. I call it searching for gold.

You approach. Remember that one-second scan in Chapter 4? You also take a quick glance at their first name and reach out to shake hands, smile, and say, "Hi, my name is [insert your name]. I don't know about you, but I set a goal to meet three people today I have never met before, and you are my first. Tell me, what brings you here today?" That's the easiest and best opener ever. Always use direct eye contact and continue smiling. Bam! That's it. You did it.

They will respond. I pinky promise. Do you know why? While they were standing or sitting alone (ahem, hiding, they don't like networking either), you just made it easy for them to meet someone new.

Now you launch into questions about them. As we talked about in Chapter 6, it's never about you. You're building rapport—Key #2.

Take your time; don't rush. Making one or two solid connections at each event is more important than running to meet many. You're working on sincere and solid connecting, not card collecting.

When you are satisfied with this new connection, hopefully, you exchange contact information. Then, you say, "I still have to meet at least two more people today." Thank them for the opportunity to have met them. Close with an agreement of either connecting within twenty-four hours or following up as agreed. Remember to write on their business card a personal attribute that stands out about the person. It will help when you move on to the ideas in Chapter 10.

That's it—not so hard, right? You just struck gold.

Feeling a bit more confident, you scan the room again, looking for your second person to connect with. They, too, are by themselves. You approach, reach out to

shake hands, and say, "I'm here to meet three people I've never met before, and you are my second.
Tell me what brings you here today?" Always make
direct eye contact and smile. Get their card and plan
to connect within twenty-four hours. Bam! You now
have two connections. More gold.

This is how you build your list. Think about the numbers. If you go to two meetings a week on average
and meet only two people max each meeting and follow up, that makes four contacts. Multiply that by fifty
weeks and you have 200 solid contacts for that year.
Attend more meetings each week with a maximum of
meeting three people at each meeting and your list
will increase exponentially.

This is pure gold!

You have established all these great connections and
don't have to pay for a list, which is usually worth zip
anyway. Most importantly, all of these connections
know people who may need to know you.

Also fundamental is keeping your goal to only two or
three connections at *any* event. It's not speed-dat-
ing. It's essential to take time to really connect with
whomever you meet by asking a lot of questions
about them with the desire to serve, *not sell.*

One time, after learning this method, my friend and client Mare Wallington was so excited after a networking event she attended that she called me on the way home. She told me she was very pumped because she had used this technique and surpassed her goal of three. She boasted about meeting eighteen people.

"No!" I said. "It's not speed dating." How effective can you be rushing down a line of people grabbing cards and running for more? How do you follow up with all these people? This is card collecting, *not* card connecting. Card collecting goes against everything I believe about successful networking.

I call my method the 3-2-1 because your strategy is to meet *only* two or three people at each event, and you can start a connection in less than one minute. You also want to make a great and lasting first impression, leaving each person feeling like they matter. This is emotional connecting. *People will always remember how you make them feel*, so make it a great, lasting first impression.

#secretofaserialnetworker

#feelingsmatter

Maya Angelou said, "I've learned that people will forget what you said, people will forget what you did, but people will never forget how you made them feel."

The bottom line is you may not have time to meet more than two or three before any meeting starts. Often, I will just say, "I decided this morning that at this meeting I wanted to meet two or three people I never met before and I saw you sitting/standing by yourself. My name is Anne Garland. What brought you here today/tonight?"

A question I often get is, "What if I know of someone but have never met the person formally? How do I then approach them?"

That is a great question. I would say, depending on the little I may know about them, to approach them this way: "Hi, Bob. My name is [insert your name]. I understand you wrote a book about (whatever) and I wanted to ask you about (whatever)." Or "I understand you are into (whatever) and I wanted to know more about it."

It is all about approaching someone with a desire to engage in conversation.

Most importantly, relax and have fun with it…. It's pure gold.

#searchingforgold

\#splitsecondconnections

GOLDEN NUGGET

Celebrate your success stories and share them. I would love to hear *your* success stories. Please share how this tip works for you. It has for so many people I have worked with. I may even feature *you* on my social media like I did Kathy Keegan at the opening of this chapter.

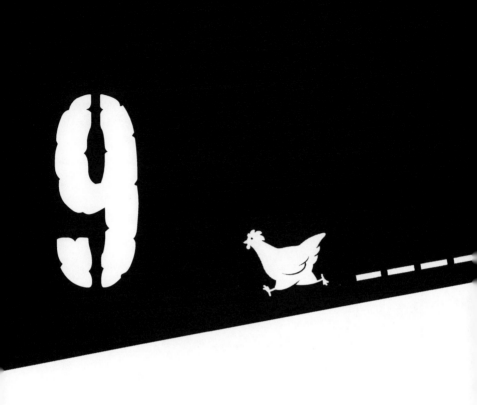

9

"Look at questions as keys on a keyring. Questions unlock doors. The bigger your keyring the more keys you have, the more doors you can unlock."

— John C. Maxwell, author, speaker, pastor

CHAPTER 9
DIGGING IN THE MINE—GOING DEEPER

ureka! You struck gold. Now it's time to find out how much more gold is there. Dig deeper—but how?

People don't like to network for three main reasons:

1. They don't know how to approach people.
2. They don't know what to say when they do.
3. They don't know how to follow up.

You now know how to approach someone using my 3-2-1 method. Now we'll look at what to say when you use it.

Below are ten of my favorite conversation starters—questions you can ask when you approach someone and begin to build rapport: Number eleven is a bonus for if you go blank at the start. Highlight the ones that make you feel most comfortable.

Remember, you are searching for a common connection, so you ask probing questions.

Let's start with three primary starters:

1. What brought you here today? (This is the easiest to lead with.)

2. What interests you about the (speaker or topic) we are going to (hear or discuss) today?

3. Did you have to travel far to get here? (Location, finding out the town they live in will be valuable in digging deeper as you build rapport.)

Stop. Oh no, what's next?

Within a minute or two, they are going to want to know what you do.

Do not throw up on them with a lot of words and share everything, including the birth of your first-born with a difficult "C section."

Now is when you *must* have ready your well-crafted five-to-ten-second response that's often referred to as *your pitch.* You must be clear, concise, and passionate. If you are all of those, you will be successful in most cases and capture their interest so they want more from you. If you add a tone of excitement, that will be contagious because the person will feel your emotion.

Many strategies exist for how to offer *your pitch* about what you do. Here is one I learned from a former coach, Chala Dincoy (see "A List" of VIP Resources in the Special Reports and Resources section). It has worked for me and will work for you:

"Do you know when (who you help) or (problem you solve). Well, what I do is (what you do to solve)."

Simple, concise, and effective.

Here's an actual example of an "intro-pitch" I use:

Do you know when I talk to *women about net-working* most of them say *they don't know how to approach someone or what to say when they do*. Well, I have a *signature tool they can learn in a minute that will put them at ease and give them confidence when they meet someone new in any situation*.

Intriguing? Yes, and I want you to be intrigued, so you will say, "Tell me more."

It's who you help, the problem you solve, and what you do to solve it.

Once you share this information, you can turn the

conversation back to them, as I discussed earlier, and lead with one of the following eight questions that show your interest in the person you are speaking with while building rapport.

4. What do you enjoy most about your work? (Find out what they do.)

5. How did you get involved in your type of work? (Show interest.)

6. What do you do outside of work? (Identify their other interests.)

7. Who would be an ideal client for you? (Learn how you can serve them.)

8. What makes you stand out among others in your field? (Gain a better understanding of their needs.)

9. If you didn't do what you are doing now, what would you like to do? (Build rapport as you show interest.)

10.   Is there someone you would like to meet who could help you in your business? (Serve them.)

11.   When you are stumped and can't remember any of the above, use the following—even if you are a man. "Where did you get those fabulous shoes?"

Clearly, one, two, and three are easy conversation starters anyone can comfortably use. As the conversation moves along and you start to build rapport, you can always ask four through ten.

If you blank out entirely and feel like a deer in the headlights, number eleven will get their attention. Ensure you really *do* love their shoes before you say it. I have found that shoes are a great equalizer among women.

I networked and connected, now what? The final step is to close out with action. There are two types of action:

Scenario 1

You want to exit and move on gracefully. You made a great connection. You exchanged business cards (always wait for them to ask you first). Don't push yourself on them. This is important—you want to build your list with people you really want to connect with who want to connect with you. Again, this isn't card collecting.

Here you want to acknowledge how excellent the connection is and thank them if it is true. Or more generally, say, "It was great meeting you." You could then say, "I would like to follow up and continue our conversation when we have more time (ask permission). Would that work for you?"

You may even feel so comfortable with this connection that you ask to take a picture together so you can post it on your social media right then and there. Super charisma points!

This type of connection is ideal for building your list.

Scenario 2

While it was an exciting exchange, the two of you really don't match in business, and you need to move on to another person. To exit gracefully, I would say, "I enjoyed meeting you, and while our businesses are in different markets, I may know someone who needs to know you (if this is true)." More than likely, they will want you to have their card.

Or you could say, "Oh, look at the time, and I have two more people to meet before the meeting starts. Thank you for your time. It's been a pleasure."

No burning bridges. You never know whom they know who needs to know you. You want to be memorable and leave a positive impression, always.

My Top 10 Conversation Starters are available for download in the Reports and Resources Section.

Guess what's next? *The* number-one mistake most people make in networking. Except you won't make it after you read Chapter 10.

#buildrapport

#meet2people

"Opportunities are like sunrises.
If you wait too long, you will miss them."

— William Arthur Ward, motivational writer

CHAPTER 10
FOLLOWING THE GOLD: DISCOVERING THE TRUE SECRET OF A SERIAL NETWORKER

say, "It ain't over until the fat lady sings."

This often-used colloquialism infers that one should not presume to know the outcome of an event still in progress.

Here's the skinny on this: If you aren't keeping in touch with your contacts, you aren't developing relationships. And if you aren't developing relationships, you aren't building your list and creating potential clients. If you aren't creating clients, you are not serving or possibly not selling, and I bet your cash register ain't ringin' either! So why bother networking or putting yourself out there?

In Chapter 1, my point was it's best to meet people *before* you need them as a resource—new friends are always great to find. And, if you establish the slightest emotional connection when you meet someone, wouldn't you want to connect with them again? The sooner, the better. Most books or articles about networking and connecting say you must follow up, with the best practice being within twenty-four hours.

Do you know why? Because *you will be remembered,* and that is a *big* way to be memorable. If the experience was positive, if you established any rapport at all and then reached out to them post-haste, you subconsciously tell them *they matter.*

In this crazy world, I find so many people caught up in social media, or their phones, computers, Kindles, etc., and not physically in front of people, connecting one-on-one. Who wouldn't want to know that those few minutes shared yesterday still meant something twenty-four hours later? Talk about sealing an emotional connection. Nothing could be more critical.

This is a significant *Secret of a Serial Networker*! The number-one secret of all. The *big* Kahuna, the *megabucks lottery*…get my drift here?

And the number-one mistake most networkers make—they don't follow up!

If you follow up, while most don't—and most people won't—you will be remembered. Think of it as a thank you note. We all like getting those, right? Someone thought enough of us to say, "Thank you; you matter." It makes you feel good, right?

I will make it super-easy. You just made two or three excellent connections at the event you attended. Your memory of them is still fresh. Following up with them is not a cold call. It's a warm lead. As soon as you get in the car, pull out the two or three cards you just received. Pull out a pen and write on the card something you found interesting about each person to use when you connect again. Write the date, event, and location on the card.

Then....

Pull out your phone. Now message, call, or email—make a re-connection right away. Call with something simple, "Hi (insert name). I really enjoyed meeting you today at (event), and I would like to reconnect and continue our conversation about (insert). Would you be open to getting together? What is your schedule next week? I'm open on (day next week)."

Do it! State a day and time right then.

Do not wait to call—the connection will grow cold, and you won't remember details.

Going home and dropping the cards on your desk in the "I'll get to that tomorrow" pile means you've missed opportunities.

Realistically, follow-up should take ten minutes and it's *done*. You won't have to think about it as you wait for their response.

Do this before you leave the parking lot.

Do you know why? Because nine out of ten people never follow up, and you want to be memorable.

Your fortune really is in the follow-up. Do not blow this important opportunity!

#followup

#callrightaftermeeting

GOLDEN NUGGET

"Nothing is more expensive than a missed opportunity."

— H. Jackson Brown

"Everything you do now is your future."

— Author unknown

CHAPTER 11
SECURING YOUR GOLD

When you meet someone at an event, it's an investment. Just like deposits in a bank, you need a safe place to keep your investments so you can track them.

Everything in Section One has led up to this point—tracking the people you talk with, gathering their information, and noting your interactions is critical to your follow-up that will ultimately lead you to clients.

How will you track them?

Many CRM (customer relationship management) programs for tracking leads and customers are available. They come with many bells and whistles and often require a fee. This software, or app in today's parlance, is where a company tracks its interactions with customers and leads; they consult it often for analysis and projections.

I want to keep it easy, simple, and free.

In every corporate sales job I've had, we tracked our customers and their information in the most minute detail. It was effective, yet time-consuming. Not to mention some managers required weekly reporting.

I want you simply to list your new contact and track them through the five stages of initial connection to becoming a client and getting paid.

These are considered warm leads. Warm leads are better than cold calls. You just met someone you connected with. In your car after the meeting, you sent a text to continue the conversation. You are on your way to build the know, like, and trust factor. If you stay in touch, I promise you it will be worth the minimal time and effort required.

The next page shows a sample of a contact tracking tool I use. I call it the Connection Sales Incubator. It's a simple way to follow your connections through the five stages.

I've also included a link to download this form in Special Reports and Resources.

YOUR CONNECTION SALES INCUBATOR

STAGE 1 Need to Connect	STAGE 2 Scheduled Meeting		STAGE 3 Gave Offer		STAGE 4 Follow-up		STAGE 5 $$ New Client	
Connect (Warm Lead)	Scheduled Inquiry	$	Gave Offer	$	Follow Up	$	Client	$
Carrie Harrison	Brenda Olsen	$1,500	Alice Woodman	$10,000	Alice Woodman	$10,000	Alice Woodman	$10,000
Brenda Olsen	Alice Woodman	$10,000	Sarah Levine	$10,000	Sarah Levine	$600	Todd Goodman	$150
Jim Turner*	Michael Mason	$10,000	Michael Mason	$10,000	Todd Goodman	$150	Michael Mason	$1,500
Alice Woodman	Sarah Levine	$10,000	Todd Goodman	$150	Michael Mason	$1,500	Sarah Levine	$600
Candy Hooper*	Todd Goodman	$150	Tanya Taylor	$600	Cathy Merkle	$1,500	Bob Cantor	$1,500
Michael Mason	Tanya Taylor	$10,000	Cathy Merkle	$1,500	Bob Cantor	$1,500	Brenda Olsen	$1,500
Kristen Warner*	Cathy Merkle	$1,500	Anita Smith	$10,000	Brenda Olsen	$1,500		
Avery Moore*	Bob Cantor	$1,500	Bob Cantor	$1,500	Avery Moore	$1,500		
Sarah Levine	Anita Smith	$10,000	Brenda Olsen	$1,500				
Todd Goodman	Avery Moore	$1,500	Avery Moore	$1,500				
Anita Smith*	Candy Hooper	$150						
Tanya Taylor*	Kristen Warner	$1,500						
Cathy Merkle*	Carrie Harrison	$1,500						
Bob Cantor								
	TOTAL Scheduled	$59,300	TOTAL Considering	$46,750	TOTAL Follow Up	$18,250	TOTAL New Clients	$15,250

Add to contacts	Move to Gave Offer or move to Nurture	Move to Follow-up or move to Nurture	Move to New Client or move to Nurture	CONGRATULATIONS!

NURTURE*

Need to Follow Up With	$	Comments
Jim Turner	$10,000	Interested next month - follow up in February
Avery Moore	$1,500	Doesn't have time right now - follow up in March
Carrie Harrison	$1,500	Money Flow Issues - Follow up in July
Kristen Warner	$1,500	Said NO - no need to follow up anytime soon
Candy Hooper	$150	Not ready right now - check back monthly
Anita Smith	$10,000	Needs coaching - check back next month
Tanya Taylor	$600	Can't attend this month - check back March
Cathy Merkle	$1,500	Family issue - not now but interested in March
	$26,750	

PROGRAM OFFERS

Offer	Cost
12 Month Coaching	$10,000
3 Week Webinar	$1,500
VIP 3 Hour Coaching	$600
Evergreen Program	$150

This is how the Connection Sales Incubator works:

There are five stages from initial connection to becoming a client.

The download Excel form will show three tabs to access at the bottom of page.

- Connect—list your new connections either from in-person or virtual meetings.

- Nurture—follow up based on your meetings.

- Contacts—everyone you meet and want to stay in contact with.

Stage 1: You connect and add names here and add their names into the contact list.

Stage 2: You schedule a meeting to connect a second time and maybe a third time. Programs and pricing have been discussed. Write cost of your program you may have discussed. It could change to another offering or stop here. Use the Nurture tab for follow-up later.

Stage 3: You will have established a rapport, and at this time, they are serious about your products and offerings, i.e., coaching, webinar, book, etc. You give a firm offer based on previous conversations.

Stage 4: Follow up and close the deal—upsell, or maybe they want a less-expensive program. Maybe no interest at this time, so you would add them to the Nurture list with notes for when to follow up again.

Stage 5: They become a client. Congratulations!

What I like about this simple system is it tracks your connections—what I refer to as gold and potential revenue to keep your eye on your financial goals.

A good CRM system will help business owners nurture relationships with potential clients. As you grow you may want to expand to a system with more bells and whistles. I like this one because it is simple to track and follow. You could use this form for each month of the year.

The Connection Sales Incubator is available for download in the Reports and Resources Section.

I want to acknowledge my good friend Terra Bohlmann. She is a business strategist who organizes entrepreneurial chaos by offering complete plug n' play systems, strategies, and tools. This is a modified version of one she offers her clients. See the "A List" of VIP Resources in the Special Reports and Resource Section on how to contact Terra Bohlmann.

#securingyourgold

GOLDEN NUGGET

My simple *free* CRM system will
track your connections (gold)

And keep you organized with an eye
on your financial goals.

It's a way of tracking your offers until
they hatch.

'12

"Those who win in networking give first, give generously, and give often."

— Author unknown

CHAPTER 12

IT'S A WRAP: WE HAVE BEEN DOING NETWORKING ALL WRONG!

What?

Throughout this book, I use the term networking. It's the term I have used for the past fifty years of my mostly corporate life. It typically fits for both men and women when they are engaging at a business meeting. Through the years, networking has morphed into meeting, connecting, gathering, interacting, etc. However, when used, everyone knows networking means all of the above. That is why I was adamant about using it in this book's title.

When I say we have been doing networking all wrong, it's coming from the school of life where I learned about the true meaning of networking.

Networking is about knowing more people.

Connecting is about knowing people more.

Every chapter in this first section is about how to connect

with people at a deeper level, building the know, like, and trust factor. To remind you what I wrote in the first chapter, I'd like to re-engineer that statement.

People won't trust you unless they like you. They won't like you until they know you.

God knows I have met thousands upon thousands of people in my lifetime. I have kept in touch with some, and with technology today, it is easier than ever to reconnect, and it is wonderful.

I know I have used my favorite quote in an earlier chapter, but it bears repeating here because it stands out in my mind most about the people I remain in contact with and aligns perfectly with what Maya Angelou said: "I've learned that people will forget what you said, people will forget what you did, but people will never forget how you made them feel."

That is a creed I highly value. The people who have made me feel good, better, welcome, etc. are the people and stories that are dear to my heart and I remember most.

My hope is you found a few "secrets" in the previous pages that you can use when it comes to in-person networking.

Here's to your continued networking success.

Now onto Section Two: Split Second Connections: 30 Worthy Tips for Making the Most of Virtual Networking

End of Section One

SECTION TWO

SPLIT SECOND CONNECTIONS: THIRTY WORTHY TIPS FOR MAKING THE MOST OF VIRTUAL NETWORKING

"The power of visibility can never be underestimated."

— Margaret Cho, comedian

INTRODUCTION
A BRAVE NEW WORLD—VIRTUAL NETWORKING

This section focuses on *you*, the professional who wants to be visible to your online market because you have a message the world needs to hear. In the following pages, you will see you have the power to go from the sidelines to center stage and become the star you were meant to be by sharing your unique gift.

My goal is to help you feel more comfortable in this brave new virtual world. The following "Thirty Worthy Tips" will be a great reminder if you have forgotten a few, and hopefully, you will discover two or three new ideas.

Most importantly, whether you are an introvert or an extrovert, I want you to be more at ease when online to help take the work out of networking.

It really can be fun, even virtually!

While the world has shifted to online networking to develop social and professional connections, I claim in-person networking is still alive and will continue because humans require one-to-one contact. We are wired that way.

Fortunately, we now have two powerful ways to network: in-person and online.

The good news for virtual networking is you can be a self-made TV star from anywhere by mastering your coveted square right from your computer or phone. (Your square? You know, the tiny square you occupy during a Zoom meeting or event. Remember, it's your space, your stage—own it.) For many, online communication is an opportunity to reach more people than they ever could before, but for many, going virtual is more critical than convenient for health, safety, and sanity reasons.

The following Thirty Worthy Tips look at the similarities between in-person and virtual connecting. Eighty percent of virtual networking is the same as in-person networking, with some crucial, nuanced differences you need to know. I will share precisely what you need to master.

When I was working out of my Fifth Avenue office for BASF, a Fortune 100 company where I created high-level events for clients, I worked with a notable NYC branding agency, The Moderns. Janine James, the founder, dubbed me the "pollinator." I attribute my networking success to engaging with people, mostly in person first, and then following up on the phone.

During my career in sales and marketing, I traveled a lot, always connecting people with one another when the opportunity presented itself. It gave me immense joy to see those connections flourish. The phone has always been my most invaluable tool—still is. Forty-five years ago, I connected by phone while sitting at my desk, or while traveling and working out of my car, I searched for phone booths at hotels and rest stops.

Of course, all that changed when the first cell phone became available for public sale in 1984—for $4,000. That was eleven years after Martin Cooper, a Motorola engineer, made the historic first cell phone call to his rival at Bell Labs, AT&T, as he walked between 53rd and 54th Streets in New York City. It was a shoebox-size portable phone that weighed two-and-a-half pounds. Can you imagine carrying that around?

Wow, nearly half a century later, my, have we evolved! Technology changed everything once again—some good changes and some not so good.

I know this to be true—we are a species that depends on other humans to survive, and when we are cut off from human contact, we usually start feeling lonely. Fear may set in, along with frustration. Being flexible and adaptable can help calm the nervous system to counter the anxiety of isolation.

I'm not a therapist; however, I know human nature. When the coronavirus pandemic hit, social distancing became one of the most important practices—and ubiquitous phrases of 2020-21—so we had to find new ways to be more visible, connecting behind a screen while building our business too. And while we've been forced into virtual connections, this new world order also has its benefits and advantages.

Therefore, I've pulled together my "Thirty Worthy Tips" to help provide insight into mastering virtual connections so you can be a more significant presence in the crowded virtual space.

Taking action and moving forward lessens fear and anxiety, so let's get crackin' on Mastering *Your* Square.

#phoneisthebesttoolstill

#masteryoursquare

'13

"Ninety-nine percent of success is showing up, even virtually."

— Anne Garland, author, speaker, master
connector

CHAPTER 13

ADJUSTING TO A BRAVE NEW WORLD, THE NOW OF NETWORKING

Are you, like so many others, "Zoomed Out"? Whether you're new to the virtual, online connecting experience or you have been networking online for a while, you'll miss critical opportunities if you don't keep up with the rules. Why? Because virtual is here to stay.

As you know from Section One, it takes seconds, not minutes, to make a first impression. It is, of course, more challenging to make that first impression with an online audience. Your viewing audience could range from one to hundreds of people, all staring at each other—and you!

What will make you stand out? How will you be seen in that tiny square, that small piece of real estate you own for a block of time? How can you sit in the front row, visible in the best way possible, to represent who you are?

You have to know how to show up. How you appear, what you say and do, can make you or break you, costing you connections, potential clients, and profits. Why is virtual networking so valuable? Why does everyone need to make peace with it, like it or not? And why do most people dislike it, whether online or in-person?

Markletic states, "Eighty percent of people join virtual events for educational purposes. The next biggest reason for joining virtual events is networking."

Networking is key to your net worth and builds business, but statistically, three out of four people don't like to network. If you don't love it, you are not alone. But it's essential, so what do you do?

I am here and ready to help.

While you will find many tips in the following pages relating to in-person networking, virtual networking will be our primary focus in this section.

Please note: The following 30 Worthy Tips are grouped into six chapters, each on a specific focus of online networking.

#networkingisyournetworth

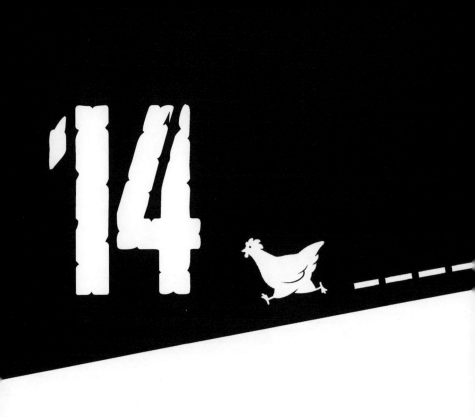

'14

"I like to connect with people in the virtual world, exchanging thoughts and ideas, when in the physical world we might never have the opportunity to cross paths."

— Demi Moore, actress

CHAPTER 14
WHY VIRTUAL NETWORKING IS SO VITAL

This first group of tips will emphasize why virtual networking is so important for you in building your business. Remember that 80 percent of in-person networking crosses over into online networking.

Tip 1: Build Your List

I emphasized this in Section One. If you are in business for yourself or working for a company, you always want to be making new connections to expand your professional network. It will help promote you more effectively, leading you to potential clients, and increase your profits.

As I like to say, "You never know whom you will meet who may know someone who needs to know you."

This statement is *big*! I will never dismiss someone based on their title or job. They could be a future client, partner, coworker, or even become a best friend who has my back. It is imperative to always be building your list of contacts and keeping an open mind about the people you meet. I will tell you how to do this in Chapter 18.

#buildyourlist

Tip 2: Gain Greater Visibility

Networking online gives you an excellent opportunity for personal brand exposure because more people see you in one shot. *You* are your brand. Before the world changed, you were primarily visible at public events with fewer opportunities to connect with many. With virtual networking, your online presence allows you to be seen and heard by the masses; however, to take advantage of this audience, you will have to be more creative in building a reputation for being someone to know.

#brandexposure

Tip 3: Sharing Your Expertise

Getting to know you in your square and what you are passionate about will give others the confidence to introduce you to people who can help you professionally and personally. Each time you speak up and share something about your profession, you offer people an opportunity to notice you in a way that may resonate with them and move them closer to getting to know you. You are gaining the "trust" factor.

#shareyourexpertise

Tip 4: Learning from Others

I have learned so much about people, life, and places by listening to others' stories and experiences on topics I may not have been familiar with. I have found there are people who feel inadequate or insecure about what to say when networking virtually. The easiest part of networking virtually is active listening. If you actively listen and ask questions of the person speaking, others online will remember you and future conversations will be easy. You don't need juicy nuggets to share—listen and ask follow-up questions. Listening builds rapport, and rapport builds trust. Trust is extremely valuable in any relationship.

#peopleareinteresting

GOLDEN NUGGET

Remember, 80 percent of in-person networking crosses over into online networking.

'15

"Technology is nothing. What's important is that you have a faith in people, that they're basically good and smart, and if you give them tools, they'll do wonderful things with them."

— Steve Jobs. American inventor, designer, and entrepreneur

CHAPTER 15
MASTERING YOUR SQUARE FROM THE TECH PERSPECTIVE

What does "mastering your square" mean?

In making a solid first impression in a virtual setting, mastering your square (your tiny box in Zoom, etc.) is where the rubber meets the road. Visibility is key. The following will help you be seen in the best light possible.

With this next group of tips, we'll talk tech basics. Here is how you set yourself up for success.

#setyourselfupforsuccess

Tip 5: Social Presence

Keep your digital image and presence current. This is a must, not a should. Look at your profiles and make sure they are error-free and clean. Complete your profiles on all your social platforms and networking organizations. If you are not active in a group, consider deleting your profile. Update your professional accomplishments and get testimonials (give them too). Think of this as your billboard.

Schedule a recurring review of these platforms for every ninety days. This is essential for your brand image.

Be aware when someone interacts with you online and shows interest. More than likely, they will jump to one of your social media platforms to see if you are worth more of their time even while you are on the call—just saying.

People do take notice and judge. Remember, you have seconds to make that first impression—everything starts here. If you wouldn't want your mother or, worse yet, your grandmother, reading something, remove it.

#updatesocialpresence

Tip 6: Headshot

What message are you sending with your photo? No skin, please. A great headshot is equally as important as your social media image. Optimize your professional appearance by having a great headshot, one that will come up on your square when you hit "stop video." A good headshot is much more effective than having just your name. Find a good photographer and get several poses or variations you can change out periodically. Changing your picture is a great way to engage your fan base and good for search algorithms.

#needagreatheadshot

Tip 7: Your Best Light

Have the light in front of you. If the light is behind you, no one can see you. And if you speak, it is very distracting, and you won't command the square as people tune you out. You will look unprofessional. Conversely, if you have too much light, you will be washed out or blinding, and that, too, is annoying and unprofessional. Close the drapery or blinds. Invest in a good halo light source. There are many inexpensive ones on the market.

If you wear glasses like me on Zoom and light reflects on them, there are solutions:

- Change the height of light to eight inches above the webcam and not even with the webcam.
- Change the horizontal position of your light.
- Don't look at the light.

- Turn up the ceiling lights.
- Use a large soft light to make reflections less noticeable.
- Use window light at an angle.
- Use blue light glasses that won't reflect light.

Get this one right, and you will look fabulous!

#therightlighting

Tip 8: Your Background aka Stage Setting

Messy or interesting? Your background will create an impression that will tell a story about you. Make it interesting. Today, you can use engaging virtual environments or create a picture that relates to your brand. Ensure it is a good one that doesn't have parts of you disappearing when you move your head since that is distracting and weird. You can also invest in an inexpensive, expandable green screen. I have one I found online that folds up into a thirty-inch circle. You can even hire a set designer who will design a physical background for you to best show your brand. The sky's the limit.

#yourbackgroundisakeytoyou

Tip 9: Sound

Invest in a good microphone. If I had to identify which tool matters most in online tech, this is it. I purchased a Blue Yeti with a Pop filter, a small investment that makes all the difference, offering you voice and sound clarity. You can use it as a desk microphone or get a boom arm to eliminate typing, tapping, or rustling paper sounds on the desk. It is that sensitive.

#goodmicrophonekey

Tip 10: Headphones

Now that you have a great microphone that enhances sound, be aware of the sound around you because it can be distracting. Kids, the TV, and dogs barking can all be annoying even from another room. A good headphone will avoid any embarrassment, and it can plug into your Yeti microphone.

Remember to turn off your portable phone or put it on mute during video calls. Nothing is more distracting than your phone ringing. If you have a landline nearby, you can dial down the ring tone, or best, pull the plug. Remember to plug it in after your Zoom call.

#nosounddistractions

'16

"Body language is a very powerful tool. We had body language before we had speech, and apparently, 80 percent of what you understand in a conversation is read through the body, not the words."

— Deborah Bull, British dancer

Understand how to use your body in your square to communicate, and it will help you connect and get noticed.

Tip 11: Head and Body Position

Here is where your visibility matters. To best maximize your square, you want your entire face in view like a headshot, period. Showing your whole face so others can see your eyes, smile, and facial expressions is critical in connecting with your audience—just like in-person connections. Do not plop yourself on a sofa, easy chair, or bed and sit way back from the camera so most of your body shows in the frame. That's fine for family gatherings, but not in a professional context. And for God's sake, if you are a guy and you stand up, keep moving. You don't want your zipper to take center stage—ever!

#connectwithyouraudience

Tip 12: Body Language

Ralph Waldo Emerson astutely said, "What you are speaks so loudly I cannot hear what you say." If you are showing more of your upper body, your posture will make a more significant impression than you realize. Sitting up straight with your shoulders back makes you appear confident. If your arms are folded, it shows more resistance to the speaker than arms open, which is a more trusting posture. And isn't trust what we are looking to achieve when building rapport?

#bodylanguagematters

Tip 13: More on Body Language

To show interest, try these positions. Lean forward as if on the edge of your seat, sit straight back, or hold your head slightly tilted and supported by one hand with fingers pointed up.

Chin stroking is a "let me consider" gesture.

Body language is a science in itself, so be sure to watch all non-verbal clues, including eye-rolling or smirks because they are truth-telling and may tell a contradictory story about how you are feeling.

Take notice when you see someone with their head

in their palm leaning on the desk with droopy eyes showing a "woe is me" gesture, indicating regret or boredom. And don't do that yourself!

#showinterest

Tip 14: Eye Contact

How are you positioned in your square? Are you looking at the computer's camera or the person on screen? It might not appear that you are looking directly at them, but when your eyes stay focused in one place, it's clear you are looking at the speaker. A good tip is to take a blank Post-it, punch a hole, and mount the paper on the screen, so the hole exposes the camera eye. I always make it a smiley face with the hole as a nose. It's easier to focus. The Post-it outlines the spot for the camera and guides your eyes toward the camera. Also, when you look down at your phone you will appear unfocused on screen. Keep the phone away from Zoom when possible. It's a distraction and rude.

About note taking: During online conferences and summits that involve many hours of teaching where workbooks and handouts require note taking, you will need to be looking down. It is expected and very different than a one-to-two-hour presentation by a speaker where it will look rude if you are looking elsewhere.

Remember to smile—smiling eyes say so much about you. Who can resist a great smile? I always zero in on the people who smile and are attentive with good lighting. I can tell they are upbeat and ready for action.

#smilingeyeswin

GOLDEN NUGGET

"Share your smile with the world. It's a symbol of friendship and peace."

— Christie Brinkley

'17

"Your personal brand is a promise to your clients...a promise of quality, consistency, competency, and reliability."

— Jason Hartman, Founder and CEO of Hartman Media Company

CHAPTER 17
GETTING PERSONAL ONLINE: NETIQUETTE

I discovered the term "Netiquette," which is a portmanteau of net and etiquette. Here is its definition: The correct or acceptable way of communicating on the internet—1993.

You just read fourteen tips to set the stage. Now it is time to focus on *you* and get on that stage.

Think of an ad you saw on TV and loved—which, by the way, sponsors have paid big bucks for in hopes of creating a memorable message. I want you to think of yourself as a brand like the product represented by that ad. What is the image you want to promote? It is time to focus on *you* and making your message memorable.

#bememorable

Tip 15: You Are Your Brand!

You are your own best advertisement. How you appear,

or show up, is important. Are you dressed well, or are you wearing a headwrap, T-shirt, or sweatshirt with opinionated and potentially offensive writing on the front? Would you go to your workplace, an in-person event, or a meeting the way you are dressed? If not, don't do it in a virtual meeting or event.

Take the time to plan how you want to be seen and received—all the time. What if you can't primp because of a family emergency, or you are ill or exhausted but don't want to miss the event or meeting? Change your shirt or top—you will feel better. If you are a woman, fix your hair and slap on some lipstick. Here is an opportunity to show you are human: be vulnerable. Type in the chat that you had an emergency or do not feel well but wanted to be there. People will understand. You will get a pass and some empathy just so long as you are sincere and don't do it often.

We form first impressions in mere seconds when we meet someone, whether online or in-person. How you look and act in those crucial first moments could dictate how others think of you forever.

As I said earlier, statistics indicate facial expressions and posture form 55 percent of first impressions; 38 percent comes from inflection and tone of voice, and only 7 percent is based on the words we use.

Remember, you are your brand.

#firstimpressionsmatter

Tip 16: Start Your Day Fresh!

To break the lazy ways of working at home in PJs and slippers, change your mindset. Exercise or walk first thing, nourish your body with a healthy breakfast, shower, and get ready for work as you used to when you left the house. This will help change your state of mind and your take on your day, and your attitude will be rosier.

#befreshandnourished

Tip 17: Dress to Impress

Yes, even online. The first and easiest way to impress is to dress like you are at an in-person networking event. I say go for being a ten. I know we all have relaxed a bit about the way we dress, even in person. But dress appropriately so you don't draw negative attention and look out of place. Make your first impression a good one, at least on top. Remember not to stand if you are only dressed as half of a ten.

#howyoudresscounts

Tip 18: Bad Hair Day?

Hair or no hair, it's your crowning glory. Please pay attention to how you are groomed since it may affect your mindset on the call and result in a not-so-positive effect on your online interactions. If you don't feel good about how you look, it will come across. Should you mention it? That has to be your call and depends on the comfort level you have with the group. Laugh about it if it can't be helped. Being vulnerable is a good thing and creates likability.

Guys, please trim and keep your facial hair neat.

#saynotobadhairday

Tip 19: Your Voice Online

When speaking, your voice, tone, and inflections account for 38 percent of the meaning people take from you, and since only 7 percent of meaning comes from the words you use, make your delivery more interesting. Avoid being monotone—add excitement and energy to your voice. Voice coaches abound since lots of theater people are always looking for extra work and have great programs to help anyone at any level. It's a great way to meet some cool, creative people while you learn to master your delivery. One of my favorite voice coaches in New York City is Monique McDonald, The Magnetic Voice. She can work with you virtually. (See the "A List" of VIP Resources in Special Reports and Resources.)

#voiceinflectioncounts

Tip 20: Your Words

Be yourself and don't *try* to impress or dominate the conversation. You will lose trust quickly. You will also likely annoy and/or frustrate the other attendees. Being confident is good, but being patient and kind go a long way.

#wordsmatter

Tip 21: Focus

Pay attention to the speaker. Everyone can see who is paying attention and who is multi-tasking. It's rude—think of the message you are sending out. If someone else at the online event wanted to connect with you, they'd wonder if you would value their time.

#befocused

Tip 22: Show Your Face

If you are on the call, show up. Putting your name or photo up there as a placeholder is the same as being invisible, and you might as well go take a nap since you appear as if you aren't there anyway. And if you have an unavoidable personal or technical issue, say so in the chat. I have seen people write in the chat room that they are eating lunch or dinner and will be listening until they finish. That's better than eating in front of everyone, but don't make it a habit.

#noscreenhiding

Tip 23: Arrive Early

I always say arriving early means you are on time. Arriving early allows you to do your tech check and resolve any issues that may come up. Nothing is more distracting than people adjusting lighting and sound, etc., after the host or speaker starts talking.

Arriving early is one of my favorite tips. Why? It is important with in-person meetings, yet even more valuable here because you have a front-row seat in front of the host/speaker. The later you sign on, the farther back you are in the gallery view. I've been on summits where 100-plus people attend, and you have to scroll using the arrows to see who else is on the call or check out the roster on chat. Arriving early, you can connect and be more visible when fewer people are online. No one understands the value of this critical opportunity of networking. It also is a time to start meeting some other early arrivals.

The next tip goes hand-in-hand with this one.

#arriveearly

Tip 24: Stay Late

This is the reverse of arriving early. If you don't exit too quickly at the end, you may get some extra time with the speaker or meet someone you didn't expect to meet. You can ask the host to stay on longer in the chat because you have a question for them or the speaker. Sometimes it works and sometimes it doesn't. Do plan some extra minutes if possible. It has worked for me when I didn't have to leave due to another obligation.

#staylatetobeseen

Tip 25: Come Prepared

Come prepared means having your coffee, tea, or

water at your desk. Read the speaker's bio and familiarize yourself with the topic before logging on. Have a pen and paper or journal ready to take notes. Being prepared includes planning a few questions and having printouts ready from the speaker if needed.

#beprepared

Tip 26: Participate

Participating does not mean interrupting. It means listening actively, asking questions when invited, and keeping your eyes up and on the screen and the speaker. Also, what can you contribute to the conversation? How can you add value? Speaking up is an excellent opportunity to be visible and get noticed. Putting questions in the chat gets you noticed. It's an amazing online tool.

#getnoticed

GOLDEN NUGGET

Netiquette is the acceptable way of communicating on the internet.

'18

"Any virtual community that works, works because people put in some time."

— Howard Rheingold, American critic

CHAPTER 18

MAKING CONNECTIONS VIRTUALLY IS EASIER THAN IN-PERSON

We have focused on the when, the what, the how, and the why of *Mastering Your Square* for greater visibility. We will now focus on how to make deeper connections when you are at a virtual meeting.

#leveragedeeperconnections

Tip 27: Making a Connection Online

Online connections are more effortless than in-person connections; however, in Section One, I discussed my never-fail 3-2-1 method for meeting someone in person. It won't work online. You need a different approach.

Engaging in any new connection starts with your mindset. Be open and be patient. It's a level playing field, and you are all in a comparable situation. When online, your eyes and ears will be your most valuable asset. You can scan the gallery to see who stands out for you.

Here is how I connect online: First, I evaluate the meeting

or event based on size—is it 100 people or a manageable few? Is the session interactive?

I look for people's smiles and listen to their voices. I look at their virtual backgrounds, which can say a lot about a person. My degree is in interior design, so I am sensitive to what people show in their backgrounds. Mostly, I look for something of common interest: books, posters, art, themes of interest. If someone appears to have a common interest, I reach out to them in a private chat. I might say, "Your photo art is interesting. Are you a photographer?" Or "I love your art" or I love something to start a conversation. It's an easy way to start a connection.

If someone has spoken and I want to meet them, I first look them up on one of the social media platforms, find out more about them, and see if there might be some synergy.

I then send a simple message in the private chat. The message is based on what I learn about the person, whether they spoke or not. I might say we have something in common, and I would like to connect.

Sometimes I will reach out to them after the meeting and tell them I saw them at (the name of the event) and wanted to reach out because (whatever the reason).

It has become more commonplace to connect this

way and gets easier the more you do it.

#virtualconnectingiseasy

Be sure to copy the chat thread—this is gold! Many people put their contact information in the chat and you can look them up on social media. If they are interesting, send a text or email explaining why you want to connect.

Before I lean into following up after the connection, I wanted to bring up the next tip.

#copychat

Tip 28: A Person's Name is Important

I said this in Section One, and it bears repeating. Understand the value of a person's name. It is the most important word in the world to a person. It's their connection to their identity and individuality. Mispronounce it or misspell it and you may see a raised eyebrow. Whether you are addressing a host, a speaker, or a new connection, take the time to repeat their name two or three times in conversation or in writing—this will score high ACP points.

#namesmatter

'19

"It takes months to find a customer and minutes to lose one."

— Renee Evenson, author

CHAPTER 19
FOLLOW-UP IN A VIRTUAL WORLD

Tip 29: The Time Is Now!

Online, you don't have to wait twenty-four to forty-eight hours to follow up with someone you want to connect with. They are accessible through the chat room, which is right at your fingertips. Reach out with a simple message about wanting to connect offline.

Also, you likely took notes on some people you wanted to connect with, so remember to follow up if you can't connect during the online event.

Remember to copy the chat thread.

I have never found anyone online who refused to connect with me. It is easier to reach out virtually than in-person.

Of course, I think two to three connections are perfect to follow up with at any meeting, even virtual. If you are doing many meetings in a week, follow up can be overwhelming. This is where most people slip up.

This is a great time to download my Connection Sales Incubator form to help keep track of contacts as I described in Chapter 11. (See Special Reports and Resources.)

You've got this. Connect ASAP.

#followupvirtually

Tip 30: Managing Warm Leads

I want to point out that all the people you meet and all the connections you make online are actually *warm* leads. It would be a shame to let them hang in the ethers with no follow-up contact. You must follow up. This is what the industry calls low-hanging fruit. You can contact these people easily, and you already have an idea of what they do and need. Even if you reach out and nothing comes from it, it is still a connection you should make and track. What would be really great is if you are not a fit, yet you know someone who needs to know them and you connect them. That's when magic happens, and you gain a forever friend.

#warmleads

#lowhangingfruit

20

"The hilarious thing about people working from home is when their work is done, they say, 'Let's go home.' Then they realize, they are already at home."

— Author unknown

CHAPTER 20

IT'S A WRAP! VIRTUAL OR IN-PERSON?

O nline networking is similar to in-person and sometimes easier.

You can make connections quickly and with a wider range of people from all over the world. However, in-person networking gives you the opportunity to create more meaningful relationships that can be memorable.

Be attentive online, be at your mental and physical best, smile, and listen.

Remember, you have a front-row seat anytime by adjusting your square.

Networking is so important to your life and business that it should not be limited to either virtual or in-person.

#makeconnectionsquicklyonline

End of Section Two

SECTION THREE

NETWORKING WITH A TWIST:
CREATING NETWORKING
EVENTS WHERE YOU ARE
THE STAR!

"Desire is the key to motivation, but it's determination and commitment to an unrelenting pursuit of your goal—a commitment to excellence—that will enable you to attain the success you seek."

— Mario Andretti, Indy 500 racing driver

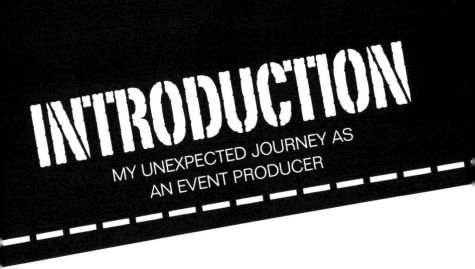

INTRODUCTION
MY UNEXPECTED JOURNEY AS AN EVENT PRODUCER

f someone asked you to name a boardgame that defined your life, what would it be?

For me, my first thought is Scrabble, where you make sense out of random letters to create a word to score points. That rings true for me. Like with Scrabble words, I'm always trying to make sense of life. And even at my age, I'm still trying to score points.

Upon reflection, I'd have to say my life has been more like the boardgame Chutes and Ladders. Climb up, up, up a ladder and encounter a chute, then down, down. Then up, up, and down again. I've learned to be resilient and patient.

In the early '90s, my interior design career, my true life's passion, ran into another chute—down, down I went again. The economy was heading into another recession.

This was my fourth recession experience and not my last

since I joined the big girl workforce upon graduating from high school. The recessions hit with my long-distance telephone operator job at Southern Bell Telephone in 1971, again with Yardley of London in 1974, and even upon graduating from Paier College of Art in 1982. Jobs were scarce in the design industry.

While in school, I became very active in the Connecticut chapter of ASID (the American Society of Interior Designers). Years later, I got elected for a national board position and, ultimately, became president of the Connecticut chapter. Thankfully, I had created another section in my Rolodex in the design industry. This was a time where my favorite "Who do you know who needs to know me?" came into play. I couldn't get a much-needed full-time job working in a design firm, so I went into business for myself.

Here is another example of how it's who you know. Through another referral, I was able to rent office space from a well-known architect, Caswell Cooke. He was a wonderful mentor, and it was a good partnership. I had my clients whom I billed, and he promoted my services as his in-house designer. His stunning office was on the bottom floor of his stately brownstone home on beautiful Wooster Square in New Haven, around the block from the famous Pepe's Pizza—a bonus perk for sure. I worked happily for two years until Caswell took a project in Saudi Arabia and moved his family. Since new clients and jobs are not always stable in the design industry, as most designers know, I finally sold out for cash.

I still miss the cherry trees blossoming in the spring, creating a beautiful umbrella canopy of pink flowers along Wooster Square that dazzle your eyes and imagination. I try to get back every year, but it's not like being right there to daily watch it unfold its magnificence.

Again, I got lucky with another referral and secured a job with benefits and a steady paycheck working for Kagan Architects in New Haven. I became their head interior designer. I loved designing high-end residential and commercial spaces. Then, *bam!* It was the late '90s, and déjà vu, another chute and another recession.

I had hoped to hold onto my job at Kagan's and be one of the last to go. However, the economy couldn't support new commercial construction. I found myself yet again thinking about unemployment lines. Or so I thought.

One critical fact to consider in networking: never burn bridges. You never know when you might come upon someone to help you cross to the other side where

242 SECRETS OF A SERIAL NETWORKER

you need to be.

The day I got laid off, one of my favorite commercial carpet reps, Tony Scaramuzza, who has since become a regional manager for his company, popped into my office to check on a job. He was bidding on one of my projects. He noticed I was visibly upset, and I shared my news with him.

After he left my office, he had made a phone call to someone about me. That evening, I received a call at home. I was offered a job with one of my design flooring contractors as their A & D (architect & design) representative, working with their clients. Brilliant marketing on their part. I decided to take it until things opened up and I could get back to design again.

That never happened as I had hoped. The universe had another plan.

Remember my favorite quote? It comes into play again: "You never know who knows someone who needs to know you." I did not know the owner of the flooring company well, yet he called me. I never knew they were looking for an A & D representative. Networking works when you least expect it. Thank you, Tony, for the referral!

My networking skills kicked back into high gear. I was

on the road again. I called on architects and designers to help them do what I had done for the past ten years, specify carpeting and flooring for commercial projects. Many of the designers I called on I had socialized with as a designer. The door was wide open wherever I went.

Through one-on-one networking, I established essential connections through serving others, in-direct selling, and creating relationships that I still maintain today.

I worked that job almost a year when another job opportunity presented itself: more money, more benefits, and more freedom. Oh, and more fun! J & J Industries, Dalton, Georgia, a commercial carpet company, hired me.

On the road again! Yippee!

The universe set me up on a four-step trajectory from graduating from design school to finding my ultimate dream job in the design industry. Stay with me here:

Step 1: I became a commercial designer of offices and commercial buildings. Recession.

Step 2: I got a job with the flooring contractor consulting to the A & D industry. I left for a better opportunity.

Step 3: I became a sales representative for J & J Industries, a carpet manufacturer working with the same design firms I had been working with at my flooring job and as a designer at networking events.

Then the magic happened. I received the best referral *ever*!

Step 4: I was in that "sweet spot," a trifecta where three circles overlap, creating a unique middle space. Sales, design, and networking. I was exceptional at all three.

Looking back, it was all divine providence. It wasn't long before I was on a new ladder, up, up, up. I owe it all to networking.

Someone thought I would be a good fit for this unique opportunity. I called. I interviewed. I got the job. Best referral ever! You never know who knows someone who needs to know you!

My dream job, my *biggest* ladder up, landed me in a beautiful Fifth Avenue, New York City office as the northeast regional manager for BASF, a Fortune 100 Company in Germany with their fibers and textile division in the United States. BASF made the nylon that went into the carpet, and the nylon was recyclable. This company was way ahead of the curve. My expertise was narrow and deep, with thousands of connections spreading all over the Northeast and beyond.

As a regional manager, I became an event planner, trainer, speaker, and manager of our BASF northeast regional team, which included reps from Boston, Washington, DC, New York City, and Philadelphia.

Each year, I would host many one-day events in major cities in the Northeast. My favorite was creating and hosting two-day retreats two times a year for some of the top architectural firms in the Northeast. I would invite twenty top architects and designers to attend. I would select the finest Relais & Chateaux hotels in my region, offering an experience that gained much praise and accolades as "not-to-miss" events. Networking was always at the core of each event.

One of my two favorite retreat locations is Blantyre, in Lenox, Massachusetts. On the first day after lunch and a two-hour meeting, I scheduled professional croquette lessons. We all wore white. I also arranged hot air balloon rides on the site—yes, I hired a balloon. I also hired a Scottish bagpiper to entertain while we made meaningful connections as we sipped champagne and Scotch concoctions on the Blantyre veranda. It was first class all the way with entertainment and an extravagant dinner to close the evening. The second day was more relaxed with seminars, and my guests would depart at 4 p.m.

Another favorite retreat location is The Inn at Perry Cabin, St. Michaels, Maryland, on Chesapeake Bay. I planned a similar format; however, this one offered horseback riding and a boat ride. Jazz musicians played while we sipped champagne on a veranda overlooking the bay at sunset, and, of course, more entertainment and a fabulous dining experience followed.

These were "A" list events, and I never had a problem with invitations being refused.

Other notable events included one-day programs at castles along the Hudson River and at the Botanical Gardens in the Bronx. If I could dream it, I would then create and produce it.

I created programs to help with the specification process about carpet, installation, and recycling carpet long before recycling became a household word.

Over my ten years with BASF, I hosted hundreds of events and met thousands of people nationwide while developing meaningful relationships by serving, not selling.

BASF does not have a consumer product to sell. The

division I worked for manufactured the nylon that is woven into the carpet. J & J Industries, my former employer, is one of BASF's product customers, and Shaw Industries is another familiar one.

Sadly, another chute was in my future.

BASF sold our division to Honeywell. I worked my same job for two more years until Honeywell sold our division to Shaw Industries, a Warren Buffet company, and one of our customers.

Yet again, I was out of a job, along with our other three regional managers.

Newly remarried, I enjoyed a brief time off before an unexpected referral called me back to New York City for an interview to work for a start-up nanotechnology company in textiles. Another ladder up, then another chute. After one year with them, as they struggled as a new company, they sold my contract to one of their suppliers. And, in 2008, the world crashed—another recession. I finally decided I was done with corporate. Period.

Relying on my resources and armed with a passion for planning outstanding events, I launched Anne Garland Enterprises, LLC, as my umbrella company and added The Idea Circle for Women, where I focused primarily on women. I haven't looked back.

Years before this, I had been bringing women together for Girls' Night Out events, and my well-known Girls' Goals at the Gris (at Griswold Inn, Essex, Connecticut) has been an annual January event that continues.

Near the end of 2008, a good friend, Nancy Ottino, and I collaborated and created an all-day conference event for October 2009 called The Reinvention Convention. One hundred fifty attendees, twenty vendors, twelve seminar offerings, and twenty-six speakers on Business, Body & Health, and Spirit topics. The reviews were positive, and so many connections were made. The women attending said they appreciated this type of conference that offered so many seminars of interest. It was an opportunity for so many speakers to share their voices and messages, giving them visibility.

Nancy moved on, and I continued producing these big conferences for four more years while offering other creative events for women, some of which continue to be annual.

Even with my journey through the years, climbing up ladders and tumbling down chutes, and then back up ladders again, I owe my successes to networking and referrals. Networking is the reason I have never slowed in moving forward, following my true passion of being creative in design or planning events and experiences for others personally or professionally.

We all seek that *wow* factor. That is my challenge with each event I produce. "Always expect the unexpected!"

I can't wait for you to read my "Magical Mystery Tour" at the end of this section—it truly is the secret ingredient to every one of my events.

#alwaysexpecttheunexpected

"An event is not over until everyone is
tired of talking about it."

— Mason Cooley, American aphorist

CHAPTER 21
CREATING NETWORKING EVENTS WHERE YOU ARE THE STAR!

I have been connecting people for years by creating successful networking events. You, too, can create exciting and memorable events. Anyone can duplicate my skills by learning a few basic steps while starting their planning.

Creating your own networking events can be fun and profitable, and you will be in control as well as being the star of the show! People will remember you—and isn't the goal visibility? As I pointed out in the previous sections, we all know the value of connections and being memorable.

Taking you back a few decades to my Yardley of London years, here is a perspective on bringing people together based on the popular Three Dog Night song "One" from 1969. You Boomers will remember it. They say one is lonely but so is two. I don't believe this! I think that when two people get together, it's a party. You have been to a restaurant. When you check in, often you say your name and a party of two, so two is a party. And everyone knows at least two people. Each of those people knows at least two people and so on. Here is where your networking connections begin. With today's social media reach, a party of two can quickly grow to a party of fifty, one hundred, or more in no time.

Webster's New World Dictionary defines "party" in many ways. However, my favorite definition is: "A group (number of persons) meeting together socially to accomplish a task." A task is a goal or result.

Every event planned has a goal or an objective, whether it is a seminar, workshop, a corporate event for a sales team, or a birthday party, even coffee for two.

#youarethestar

This third section offers seven steps to consider when planning and producing your own events, where you are the star. These are the seven steps:

Step One: Planning a Successful Event: Determine Your Goal

Step Two: What's in It for Them?

Step Three: It's All in the Details!

Step Four: Networking at Events

Step Five: What Is the Takeaway?

Step Six: Show Me the Money!

Step Seven: Plan-Do-Review

22

"An archer cannot hit the bull's eye if he doesn't know where the target is."

— Author unknown

Why do you want to bring people together by hosting an event?

Yes, yes, you want to be the star of your show. I get that. However, your attendees want to feel it's about them, not you. You wooed them there by selling a problem you will be solving or an experience they imagined. Based on your invitation and marketing, they plan to walk away with information to help move them forward in their lives or business—unless this event is pure entertainment with no call to action. What are their expectations?

Is your goal, ultimately, to sell a product or service? I tell people who proclaim they hate to sell that we are all selling something. Even doctors and hospitals are selling their services, and they, too, are competitive and want to be visible.

Are you planning to be the speaker or have other

speakers motivate or train your guests? Or both?

Maybe you want a panel of experts to exchange ideas or solve problems. All of this is your *why* for having people attend your event. It is the message you want to present to them, so they remember you as the connector...which leads us to the second step.

#determineyourgoal

23

"Day, n. A period of twenty-four hours, mostly misspent."

— Ambrose Bierce, American short story writer

CHAPTER 23
WHAT'S IN IT FOR THEM?

You now know what you want. What do your attendees want?

Why would people take time out of their busy schedules, leave their families, and maybe pay money to share time with you? What value will you bring into their lives that would make them willing to spend time and money to join you?

Put yourself in their shoes. There are only so many hours in a day, and everyone feels pulled in a thousand directions. You will want to design your program to be packed with interest, and to be experiential.

Consider the niche. With so many networking opportunities out there, both in-person and online, how will you stand out?

Will it be a program for a specific target market, or will it be broader in scope to meet the needs of the masses? Knowing the answer to this question is critical because it will help you define the size of your gathering, the type of location you want to consider, and your primary theme.

Will you need a quiet space or a more social setting? I have often held small gatherings where I used the conference room in the newest hip restaurant, and it became very intimate. Everyone had a chance to get to know each other and walked away feeling satisfied with the time well spent and meaningful connections made.

Conversely, I have had blowout events where, for example, I rented the ice-skating rink at Rockefeller Center along with a famous restaurant overlooking the rink. I brought in a few musicians and enjoyed a memorable late afternoon/evening with 150 guests. It was a new experience for most of the attendees—many of whom had lived in New York City for years but never ice-skated there. I held this event a second year with 300 guests. It was equally fun and memorable, especially during the Christmas holidays.

People could not wait for the next event and asked to be on the "A" list for future invites. That was one way I created my client lists. I built my reputation of "Not to Miss" events with the Architectural and Design community creating memorable experiences.

#whatsinitforthem

GOLDEN NUGGET

Go for the best venue your budget
will allow since your goal is to impress
them with the experience—which
leads us to our third step.

24

"Nothing can cure the soul but the senses, just as nothing can cure the senses but the soul."

— Oscar Wilde, Irish writer and poet

CHAPTER 24
IT'S ALL IN THE DETAILS!

Details are where magic reigns, and it's the one area that can set you apart from the pack. Details are when all of the senses come into play, starting with sight—the visual appeal of the food, the surroundings, the table settings, the sounds, the scents, and the windows' views.

The Venue and Setting

The environment makes the same first impression as if you were meeting someone for the first time. You have seconds to make that first impression. Do not underestimate its power.

The subtleties of the environment affect how a person feels. As an experienced interior designer, I understand the effects an environment can have on a person's mood. Consider this as you attend your next event.

What emotion does the setting evoke in you?

What emotion do you want to evoke in your guests?

You can control this. You will want to consider lighting and how bright or dim the surrounding needs to be. That will depend on the mood you want to create in the space, the time of day, and the audience.

I want you to consider the difference in how you felt when you entered a corporate boardroom against entering your favorite fine restaurant's dining area.

All of these considerations relate to emotion and the experience you want your guests to feel.

#locationlocationlocation

Food, Glorious Food

Let's venture into food and presentation. Taste is essential and can be the most scrutinized factor of an event. Like it or not, it's true. If people don't like the food, it will be downhill, regardless of your other details. Sorry to say, it will not matter how great the speaker or other details are—all your guests will remember is the wrong food and the wrong venue.

I remember attending a long-anticipated seminar with a highly acclaimed speaker. Before his presentation, we spent time networking. The buffet table offered a light fare of hors d'oeuvres and vegetables poorly presented. It was more like a parents' night at school. It seemed to me that the facility food staff had forgotten to plan and had to send out for food from a big box store at the last minute. It was awful!

As much as I liked the presentation, what stands out most in my mind is the poor food. Thank goodness there was wine. The moral of this story is: Know the quality of the venue's service and food before you commit to using their space. Please *do not* leave it to chance. Ask for a tasting appointment, especially if it is a big event. If it is a restaurant, go yourself and try their food. Always read their reviews where they rate the environment, food, service, and price. That is a good guide next to having first-hand experience.

When I worked in New York City, I hired an event planner specifically for venues and often went to tasting parties where the restaurant would serve drinks and food. It was not only marketing for the restaurant, but it was also networking. Great times and great memories followed. Ask for a tasting.

Before my New York City days when I worked for the architectural office in New Haven, Connecticut, we hosted weekly "lunch-and-learn" events that I organized where industry suppliers came in and presented their products and services so we could specify their products on upcoming jobs. It was a great example of hosting an event because it involved networking while promoting a product or service on a small scale. It was a win-win for the supplier and us since often we were too busy to leave the office for lunch. Sadly, we tended to judge the supplier host by the food they presented. If we liked the food, we were more likely to invite the presenter back, and, of course, we were more likely to specify their products for our clients. Food quality and presentation is important, so please consider its value when planning.

#goodfoodmatters

Sound

The next consideration is sound. Be aware of acoustics and sounds in a room and how sound waves interact in a space. Have you been to a diner or restaurant with hard surface tables and floors? Conversations and plates rattling can be deadening, bouncing around with nothing to absorb the sound waves. Carpeting and acoustic ceiling tiles will help. Tablecloths will also help absorb sound. Sensitivity to sound is essential if using a microphone. I sometimes find a microphone can be overbearing and less intimate. However, make sure everyone can hear the presentation and speaker.

Are you using music or none at all? Will the size of the group and area require amplification for the speaker?

Will adjoining rooms be noisy and distracting? All these are important to consider when it comes to sound.

Know all your tech needs and check with the facility about what they offer. Not all venues are updated with the latest technology. You may need to bring in a sound and tech company to run your event. Be as professional as you can afford. You want your audience to have the best experience possible, including good visibility to the stage or front of the room where the speaker is positioned.

#acousticssmatter

Olfaction/Smell

Olfaction is the special sense through which smells (or odors) are perceived.

Often overlooked and no less important is the sense of smell. Please consider this as well. Aromas from an Italian restaurant create a very different emotion than those from a bar-b-que place. If you are a garlic lover like me, you can almost taste the garlic as you enter the restaurant, which is a different scent from your local fish market.

Keep in mind that carpeting can harbor odors, too, so you want to check out the venue and the space where you will be hosting. Is it musty, a dark space, or does it smell of liquor? These may seem minor issues, yet they do play with emotions.

If you consider an intimate space, you might enhance the room with flowers, fragrant candles, or oil diffusers, creating a different feeling. Often, a particular scent can trigger a pleasant or unpleasant experience or memory for a person. For instance, think of apples baking in the oven. Doesn't that conjure an excellent thought of a time when a relative made an apple pie that just melted in your mouth? How does that make you feel at this moment? Now, imagine when you smell cooked hard-boiled eggs. A very different emotion surfaces.

Any of these considerations can set the mood for a connection, positive or negative, depending on the desired effect, your event objective, and the people involved. Be aware; do your homework.

When it comes to addressing the senses, the bottom line is to provide your guests with a distinct set of positive experiences, and that is the most crucial aspect of the event where you tie it all together, using the various senses as mood enhancers or mood changes, no matter how small or big your gathering.

I remember hosting an event for forty-plus architects and designers in Philadelphia at this new, hip restaurant. The architectural firm that designed it created several pods—egg-shaped round capsules for six to eight people to sit. These capsules were an off-white plastic material, otherworldly. What was fantastic as we sat inside is that we could adjust the lighting color and brightness to change the mood of the inside space. It was fun and different for my guests, an experience they talked about for a long time, and the food tasted remarkable.

With sensitivity in planning, paying attention to

all sensory experiences will keep your guests interested and involved, even in the most subtle of ways.

We've addressed the venue and sensory details. Next, let's talk networking!

#detailsmatter

25

"The value of networking is not measured by the number of people we meet but by the number of people we introduce to others."

— Simon Sinek, author and inspirational speaker

CHAPTER 25
NETWORKING AT EVENTS

etworking at events starts way before the event. You start with invites either by email or through social media channels. You can customize social media platform tools to target your specific niche for invites. Consistency in your campaign is key.

My best results for inviting attendees come from my email list and Constant Contact, an email marketing platform. Make sure you keep your list current.

I set up a specific event group page for those who register, and I make it interactive *before* the event so people can start connecting. I engage those participants to build the excitement before everyone meets in person. At the conclusion of the event, I will promote an "Afterglow," which is an online after party for those who want more networking to share photos and stories; it's a way to continue being interactive and fun.

If you want your event to be successful in creating a buzz

of energy, it *must* be interactive. Create a way for everyone to get involved, allowing for exchanges among your guests and speakers so they get to know each other. Otherwise, you may lose them. They may never even realize why they feel blasé about your event.

Even though we are social creatures, networking doesn't just happen. Whether you are an introvert or an extrovert, you will need to encourage your attendees to connect, and it can happen in a variety of ways.

I have organized various ways of informal networking at the beginning of events to create connections so even the shy and introverts will want to return again and again.

I have many creative ways to bring people together. Here are two I have used that were successful.

For a group of thirty or less, I arrange for everyone to receive someone else's nametag so they can talk to others to find the person wearing theirs. Usually, when creating this, I purposely pair up people who share something in common. This makes for a fun connection and fun experience overall, kind of an entrepreneurial "matchup date" if you will.

At another networking event, we only put first names on the guests' nametags and they were not to ask anyone what they do or what their business was. They could only ask questions about interests, family, life, etc. Most said it was difficult not to ask what people did for a living, which I think made it an even more interesting exercise.

Creative connecting exercises can add to the overall experience at the start of most events. Think outside the box!

The following format works great for smaller networking retreats or business seminars with a group of fewer than twenty-five:

At the opening meeting, after the welcome, housekeeping, and review of the program and agenda, I ask each person to take a minute to introduce themselves by name and location and to share something unusual about themselves. You would be amazed by the connections that result from that question alone. It is a great connecting opener. I have seen strangers connect over having twins or the same type of pets, etc.

Then, I ask guests to comment on what they hope to get out of the seminar or which question they most hope will be addressed based on their interests in the program.

Whatever particular niche you are presenting on, as the expert, you can then pepper those answers throughout the seminar.

Have a marker board available and note each person's name and question. This is an excellent opener after you welcome the group, and it lets them know you are actively listening and personally interested in them and their needs. At the close of the event, go back to each question listed on the board and make sure you have addressed them all. You would be surprised how that ties everything together and makes you the expert.

This fantastic tool adds value to everyone's experience and can help them feel connected to you, the speakers, and each other.

Making connections is vital to building the know, like, and trust factors, and as you become more comfortable helping to forge relationships, you will become more valuable in being the ultimate connector, which leads us to Step Five: What Is the Takeaway?

#knowlikeandtrust

#setupagroup

26

"The intense happiness of our union is derived in a high degree from the perfect freedom with which we follow and declare our happiness."

— T. S. Eliot, poet, essayist

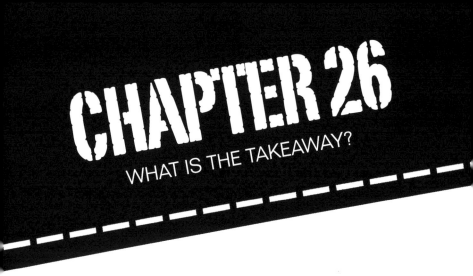

CHAPTER 26
WHAT IS THE TAKEAWAY?

he takeaway is where the emotional impact of your program will be evaluated. What were your attendees' final impressions? Did you satisfy their needs and interests? Did you meet your objective? Did you deliver your branding message? Your real job as a facilitator or networking host or speaker host is to inspire the audience. The speaker(s), if not you, and the details of your production should create an enriching experience offering value and tangible results. What will attendees remember most about the time they shared with you? Ask for feedback on the efforts you put forward. I suggest a simple questionnaire for attendees to complete right before they leave to help measure your success and their happiness. You ask them, "How did I do?"

Here are a couple of guidelines for the questionnaire:

- Keep the questionnaire simple and easy to fill out with no more than five questions.

- Use an onsite questionnaire to collect their response before they leave.

- If you wait until after the event to send out a questionnaire, you can expect the percentage of responses to be reduced. People may not remember the details or may be too busy to respond the longer you wait.

The day of the event is the best time to get the most honest response. Regardless of the size of your event, you can offer the chance to get a free lunch or ticket to your next event or some incentive for taking the time to fill out the form, and then randomly select one of the finished questionnaires, similar to a raffle. Play with this and have fun. If you want to send the questionnaire to attendees immediately by email the same day or evening, your response will be less effective.

Here are some sample questions to consider. For the first two or three questions, ask participants to respond on a scale of one to five, five being strongly agree and one being strongly disagree.

- I received valuable information.
- My expectations were met.
- The event exceeded my expectations.

The following two will be short responses:

- What is the most powerful message you heard?
- Which topics would you be interested in in the future?

Yes and no questions work too.

- Would you recommend us/me to a colleague? (circle) Yes No
- I am interested in attending more events (circle) Yes No

Here is another add on:

- If you valued today and your experience, I would welcome your testimonial to use on my website or social media. Thank you.

The last request is asking for name, company, email address, and phone number.

With this type of questionnaire, you acquire updated contact information on your attendee. You will discover strong candidates with whom you will want to set another appointment to share additional information on your product or services. Isn't that the goal? Questionnaire information can be invaluable.

This leads us to the next step—probably the single

most important step in making your connections count.

#questionnaireswork

#finalimpressions

"Success is not a destination. It's a journey."

— Zig Ziglar, American motivational speaker

CHAPTER 27

SHOW ME THE MONEY!

ach of these steps has led you to the most critical point—your connections. The planning and execution of the event is leading you to the bullseye.

Your bullseye is your CTA—call to action—and follow-up. It's where you tell the audience about the role they can play after they leave your talk or event and how you might take them to the next steps of learning.

Are you promoting a product, book, or another program that piggybacks on the day's event? You could outline your CTA on a one-sheet handout with information that directs attendees to your website or landing page. When there, the simplest example of a call to action is "Buy now!"

With regards to follow-up, if you collected a questionnaire or sent one, reach out and thank your attendees with a reminder of the event, the experience, and the call to action with some sort of time limit.

You will want to keep a separate tracking sheet of your attendees with notes and any follow-up needed. In Section One, I presented you with a tracking form, the *Connection Sales Incubator*. It's a great tool. You can download a blank form from the link in our Special Reports and Resources section in the back of the book. If you missed it, you can see sample of it in Chapter 10.

It is as simple as that!

#showmethemoney

#followup

#calltoaction

Our last and final step is what I call Plan-Do-Review. It is an invaluable assessment I use for each of my events from the beginning to the end.

"First comes thought; then organization of that thought, into idea and plans; then transformation of those plans into reality. The beginning as you will observe, is in your imagination."

— Napoleon Hill, American author

CHAPTER 28

PLAN-DO-REVIEW

A t your event I want you to have planned well so you can relax, enjoy your guests, and have fun. If *you* have fun, your attendees will have fun.

Our last final step:

After-event marketing, or what some event planners call the postmortem, is more than just evaluating your event and questionnaires or sending a thank you note or even making phone calls—all of which are essential for establishing your brand. More importantly, you have established an invaluable database of fans who, if you have given them an unforgettable experience, may return to your next event and bring their friends. This not only builds brand loyalty, but it produces more connections and business. Networking plus connections equals more clients. Clients are paying customers. I always say networking is your net worth. It is all about making the right connections to meet the people who will help your business grow.

I have found that creative events and diverse programs are invaluable tools for meeting people who then lead me to other people and so on.

It is true that the most effective and memorable events, no matter how small, are productions or shows. You, as the producer, must take responsibility for the details of producing a good "show."

With some creativity and proper planning, you, too, can create successful networking events that generate great results. Use the steps in this chapter to create a framework for a successful networking event. Determine your objectives, focus on the details, and ensure an enriching experience for your audience to make your connections unforgettable through this medium.

On the next page, I have created a document you may find helpful. It's called Anne's Plan-Do-Review: 20 Quick Steps for a Successful Networking Event.

Note: In the back of the book is a list of Special Reports and Resources that contains the link address to download this document. Enjoy!

#plandoreview

Anne's Plan-Do-Review: 20 Quick Steps for a Successful Networking Event

As an expert with more than thirty years of event planning experience in creating and producing corporate and my own personal events, I get a lot of calls to help entrepreneurs. One of my secrets for networking is hosting events where the host is the star!

I have mastered bringing together both extroverts and introverts and creating a space for each type of person where they can network and get results.

While event planning and execution can be a lot of work, it draws crowds, whether it is in-person or virtual. The following steps are some of the many considerations in planning.

PLAN

1. Define your *purpose, your why.*

2. Define your target market. Know your niche and whom you serve. (Hint: It's not everyone.)

3. Choose between *in-person* and *virtual*.

4. Set a date, time, and length for the event. Consider holidays and scheduling conflicts.

5. If in-person, how many attendees?

6. Will you need team support? Who and how many?

7. If in-person, select your location, venue, and food options.

8. Consider and execute budget negotiations and contracts. (Even virtual events can cost money.)

9. Plan the program, including speakers, handouts, vendors, sponsors, and photographer.

10. Understand your audiovisual requirements for both in-person and virtual events.

DO

11. Create graphics and social media marketing, a Facebook group event page.

12. Create a registration process for before the event, and if it is an in-person event, map the flow of the event.

13. Send reminders to registered attendees one month and again one week before the event, the day before the event and then again on the day of the event.

14. On the day of the event, serve your attendees. Everyone is a VIP!

15. Get testimonials the day of the event. They can be live or written.

REVIEW

16. You did it. Congratulations! Honor *yourself* for your efforts.

17. Follow up with your team, attendees, vendors, and sponsors. (You can have virtual sponsors.)

18. Post photos on social media.

19. Review what worked and what could have been better.

20. Book your next event and keep the momentum going!

Chapter 29 is one of my favorite chapters to share with you. Are you ready to learn my secret ingredient to all of my events? Keep reading.

"Magic is believing in yourself. If you can do that,
you can make anything happen."

— Johann Wolfgang von Goethe, German poet,
playwright, novelist

CHAPTER 29
A MAGICAL MYSTERY TOUR EXPERIENCE

Today, everyone is talking about the *experience*. Experience is something I have aimed for and mastered for years in creating magic for my attendees at my events.

> *"The idea of networking can feel daunting and uncomfortable…until you attend an event led by Anne Garland. With a flair for creating vibrant events with dynamic speakers, a penchant for empowering others, and an ever-warm welcome, Anne transforms networking to a way of connecting (personally and professionally) that is fun, engaging, and something you can't wait to do again…and again."*
>
> — Nancy Cohen, Connecticut

NEWSFLASH: I'm pulling back the curtain—I have *never* shared this exercise with anyone. I use it when creating any event, and truly, it is my secret ingredient for every one of my events.

Suppose you already do events or are thinking about producing your event. In that case, you have an excellent opportunity to bring people together to network where you are the host featuring a speaker, or you will be the featured speaker, and you are the star where the light shines only on *you!*

This chapter alone is worth the price of this book!

"Magical Mystery Tour." The title is straight from the Beatles' 1967 song.

With every event I create, I want to take you away for an unforgettable experience. The magic is in the *details!* And I want to share with you how I get there.

I want *you* to stand out from the sea of sameness and set yourself apart from all others when hosting your events. Why? Because many people like me want to be part of an experience when we attend an event. We want the energy and the magic *and* the message being delivered not to be just a ho-hum experience.

In Chapter 28, I gave you my "Anne's Plan-Do-Review: 20 Quick Steps for a Successful Networking Event." It is a quick view guide that may help you in planning your events.

As I outlined earlier in this section, good event hosts and planners cover most of the planning basics, and if you are also the speaker, it adds another layer. What is missing is understanding the genuine emotion of *why people* leave any event feeling full and inspired or not.

I do my Magical Mystery Tour exercise with every event, no matter how big or small.

It is critical to understand how your guests will feel throughout the event. You start with imagining *yourself* as the attendee; then you anticipate every experience you may encounter from your arrival to your departure. The purpose of this exercise is to allow you to plan every possible scenario and detail so there will be few hiccups or complaints. No event planner is perfect, yet this exercise may help limit stress in planning and execution.

The Plan: We, Together, Are Going to Create a Sample Event

First, define your purpose and your why. Will the event be virtual or in-person? Determine whether it is a personal or business event. Intimate or large. Informal or more formal.

Who is your audience and target market?

Suppose you have decided it is in-person; what day of the week will you choose? Weekends usually will cost more because you have to pay the help for weekend service, etc. Will you be offering breakfast, lunch, or dinner? Dinners are the costliest.

The setting and a venue selection will be important and will add a certain emotion.

Will you be the main speaker promoting your product, services, book, or a combination? How many people will you need for team support?

Who will do the marketing and promotion (i.e., graphics, social media, etc.)?

As you can see, all decisions need to be made early.

The Event

Let's assume the event space has a maximum capacity of fifty people, and it's at a lovely location you have already visited where the setting overlooks beautiful water views. Settings are important.

We will plan a lunch buffet, which is usually the most cost-effective. We will prepare for 35-50 people max, which will cover the cost of the room, food, etc. that fits your budget for the price you need to quote to attend and your ROI (return on investment). You will be promoting a program, and you will be selling your book. You will have someone introduce you and help with reception and back-of-room sales. You will speak for ninety minutes. It will be a three-hour event.

Are you ready to join me on our magical mystery tour?

My process starts with us being seated, getting comfortable, and closing our eyes. We imagine our guests have accepted our invitation with details of time, location, parking, whether they have prepaid for the event or will pay at check-in and are now departing for the event. However, they find transportation there, our guests arrive at the venue location. We can't help them with how their day went or the traffic; however, we want their arrival to be welcoming and accessible. The water views can help. Always be aware of any emotions they might be feeling throughout this process. That is key. If you can recall an event similar to this one as a reminder, it may help with projecting moving forward through this process.

The guest finds the venue based on your detailed invitation.

Suppose your guest has never been at this venue before. What is their first impression upon arrival? What is the curb appeal, as they say, when buying a house?

How is parking? Is it valet or self-parking? If they have to pay for parking, make sure you state that on the invitation: Paid parking available near the venue or parking free at the venue—each will set different expectations.

If it is inclement weather, how will that affect their mood with parking and entering the venue? How far is the walk to the main entrance? I think about those details, and you might want to also.

They enter your event:

How is the entrance? Is it attractive? Would flowers be a nice touch? Will we have someone greet them, or will signage inform them where to go? Or do they have to find their way on their own and ask around? How would that make you feel?

Is there a coat check, or is it not needed? Do our guests go directly to a registration table?

How is that experience for them so far?

How will they be greeted at registration? Is it an easy process? Like most four- or five-star hotels, they train their staff for a pleasant reception experience so that guests will arrive with ease and simplicity of registration to set a positive start to their experience.

We need to think about other details. Are walk-ins welcomed? Do they have to pay upon arrival and need a receipt? Will they get a name tag? For 35-50 attendees, one person checking people in may cause a back-up at registration; however, two would be ideal. How is that experience for them?

Are they still wondering what to do with their coat or locating a bathroom? More support for your team: a friendly greeter or two could help give information about seating or maybe have it addressed at check-in. If we want it informal, that's OK; they can mingle, network, select their seat, and put their coat on the back of the chair if they have one.

Room layout, tables, and seating for 35-50:

Plan 6-7 to a table. Any reserved seating needing reserved signs?

Sometimes, if you have ample space, you may want to put fewer people at a table and use more tables to make the room look fuller.

- How are the room and table layouts? Tight space or room to move?

- Where are you, the speaker, being placed so all people can see you?

- Does the venue offer a stage or platform so you are higher than the people seated? Will you need to rent one?

- Do you need a podium or table for your presentation?

- What about your audio-visual needs? What does the venue supply?

  - Will music or entertainment be happening: upon arrival, during your presentation, when? Who will run that? How are the acoustics?

  - Where is the bar location, or is it service from wait staff? People may want to order drinks during lunch. Will the bar take cash, or will they need tickets and who sells the tickets?

- Are there sponsors and exhibitor tables to visit? If so, how are they being displayed and accessed? When do exhibitors arrive and break down?

- Will there be networking in the beginning before the program or afterward? I always arrive early and stay late for the best networking when I am a guest.

- Do you give out an agenda or schedule? Will there be meeting handouts? Do you supply a notebook and pen to take notes? Any attendee gifts or sponsor gifts being offered?

- Did you decide on vendors/sponsors? What are you charging? How many can fit the space? Remember, we are promoting *you* as the speaker. Sponsors are always good, especially if they complement your program and book. If you have vendors, they should enhance the day's experience without competing with your offerings and book sales.

Serving Lunch

A double-sided buffet is best for ease of flow. Flowers on the buffet and guest tables? Will the venue supply any?

Do we want to serve dessert with lunch or after you speak? Always offer tea and coffee, even if you will provide dessert later.

Allow enough time for lunch, and if you have vendors, it will give people time to visit them before you speak.

Program Starts and Ends

Someone introduces the speaker—that's *you*! Time to shine! Who introduces you? Do they have a unique role or relevance to this meeting in any way?

You thank guests, sponsors, and vendors if applicable for attending.

You present for one hour with Q & A.

You rock your presentation! You dazzle, inspire, and inform. Congratulations!

It is now the close of your talk. You have 15-20 minutes to wrap up.

You have a call to action (CTA). Make your new program offer and plan to sign books in the back of the room.

Announce your questionnaire—3-5 quick questions filled out. Who will collect them?

Maybe this is when you offer a raffle to one of the guests chosen from the questionnaires handed in.

At the close of your talk, we will need at least two people in the back of the room, well informed of your program offer, to answer questions. You will create a one-sheet program outline and registration form; it could be all-in-one. You are selling books, so it would be ideal to have someone do the sales transaction while you are seated at a table nearby signing and talking to guests.

Depending on the time of the event, will there be a

bar open offering cocktails? Will coffee, tea, and a light dessert be at a separate buffet table as promised to stimulate more networking.

At the close of the event, it is a fabulous time to get video testimonials. Who will do that?

Everyone is joyful, the experience was wonderful.

Departing, what does that feel like for them?

I believe you are getting the concept of my process of imagining *every* detail possible from arrival to departure and all the emotions your guests could experience in-between as an attendee during this event.

It will vary from different venues and programs.

Again, I want to express the *experience and emotions you want your attendees to walk away feeling.*

This concept is my Magical Mystery Tour. Use this process with every event, and you will be a standout and memorable!

Good luck. You can open your eyes now.

How do you feel? Exuberant, ready to rock and create your event?

Let's GO!

30

"Whatever you do, do it well. Do it so well that when people see you do it, they will want to come back and see you do it again, and they will want to bring others and show them how well you do what you do."

— Walt Disney, American entrepreneur, animator, writer, voice actor, film producer

CHAPTER 30
IT'S A WRAP! YOUR TIME IS NOW!

U nderstanding your goal and objective for producing an event is critical. Being organized and planning ahead will save you a lot of headaches, heartaches, and money.

Use the Plan-Do-Review outlined in Chapter 28 as a guide.

There are many people who are members of that famous radio station, WIIFM, "What's In It For Me." If you are clear on your content and message and you promote your event with the gift of a problem you will solve, people will give up their time if they believe it will fulfill their needs. This is when you have done a great job of marketing, promotion, and informing your target market of the intended outcome.

I will say this over and over—the magic is in the details—yet you must deliver your promise and the problem you will solve.

Here's to your success in connecting people through outstanding networking events where *you* are the star!

And suddenly, you know it's your time to start something new and trust the magic of beginnings.

I hope you enjoyed this journey with me.

End of Section Three

"The currency of real networking
is not greed but generosity."

— Keith Ferrazzi, American author

A FINAL NOTE

CONNECTING, SERVING, AND ATTRACTING MORE CLIENTS

It has taken me a lifetime to write this book. I don't mean the two years with the interruption and pause due to the pandemic that has seemed like a lifetime. It has been my actual lifetime of connecting with people all over America since I graduated from high school and joined the work world up until my semi-retirement.

It has been five decades of climbing ladders and encountering chutes only to find new ladders. At every step, I have met the most amazing people and, occasionally not so nice, yet I grew from every experience.

I believe most people are good and want to contribute to helping others. That is my hope in writing this book—to help you gain more confidence networking virtually or in-person so you are able to approach anyone in any situation and connect with the people who are excited to meet you, work with you, and pay you.

Throughout each section of this book, light humor aside,

my goal has been to share with you the success I have achieved through networking throughout my work life and pass those tips along to you.

I have often been challenged to answer the question: Which is better in connecting with people—in-person or virtual when networking?

They both have pros and cons, and my answer is different for each.

Virtual networking is where you have a front-row seat and access to everyone on the call. It is a lot easier to make two to three connections virtually because you get to choose right there who you want to connect with and then reach out in the chat to say you would like to connect offline. Connections happen quickly and you take it from there. This is what I refer to as a warm lead. It's where you connect and do a quick follow-up in one swoop.

In-person networking is more challenging because you have to walk up to someone you may not know and introduce yourself, start a conversation, and then follow up. Not as easy as making a virtual connection; however, it's many times more gratifying for most people.

If we haven't learned anything else during these chaotic times, we have learned that humans, in order to survive, need connection and human touch. I believe handshakes will never go away and neither will hugs, even post-pandemic.

We have heard and read many stories about the hunger for the touch of a child or parent not living with us. We know that lack of touch affects us emotionally, which affects our emotional and physical health. And when our health is off, it affects our business, which affects us financially.

Networking, connecting—however you choose to name it—the most important takeaway is that people need people regardless of where you live in the world. And now, more than ever as we slowly emerge from chaos, we need skills to help us get and stay connected.

"NETWORKING IS ABOUT KNOWING MORE PEOPLE.

CONNECTING IS ABOUT KNOWING PEOPLE MORE."

In the following pages, you will be able to access

reports and resources that I have addressed throughout the book.

While this is the end of this book, I hope it is only the beginning for you in your new and exciting role as a more confident networker.

SPECIAL

REPORTS
AND RESOURCES

A CHARISMATIC PERSONALITY QUIZ (ACP)

HOW CHARISMATIC ARE YOU?
LET'S DETERMINE YOUR CHARISMATIC SCORE

On a scale of 1 to 5, with one being the lowest and 5 being the highest, circle the number that best represents you. Add up your numbers and at the end determine which areas you aced and in which areas you could use some improvement. This test is not an exact science; however, you may discover you are more charismatic than you realize. We often see charisma in others and not ourselves.

---

1. I am optimistic and enthusiastic about life, and I would describe my life as a glass half full.

    1   2   3   4   5

2. When first meeting someone, I ask questions to find a common interest and build rapport. I seek to find what makes the other person unique and what gift they came into this world to share.

    1   2   3   4   5

3. I am genuinely interested in what people are saying. I'm a good listener and genuinely care about others.

    1   2   3   4   5

4. I never worry about what someone will think of me and speak my mind openly and confidently.

    1   2   3   4   5

5. When I believe in something I am passionate about, I get excited to share it with others.

    1   2   3   4   5

6. Whenever possible, I like to engage in sharing stories that people can relate to as a form of connection.

    1   2   3   4   5

7. I will take risks showing people that I am vulnerable, authentic, and not perfect.

    1   2   3   4   5

8. I am kind and non-judgmental. I am open to people's differences.

    1   2   3   4   5

9. I am confident, and my voice reflects the influential expert I am.

    1   2   3   4   5

10. I am good at remembering people and their names.

    1   2   3   4   5

Being charismatic is having the power to attract and influence others.

The following are some of the characteristics that describe someone who is perceived to be charismatic:

Optimistic, positive energy, joie de vivre, charming, personal appeal, confident, authentic, passionate about something, assertive, a good communicator, a good storyteller, empathetic, influential, unusually calm, humble.

How did you score?

10 – 15

You may be more introverted than extroverted, but that is not a bad thing. You just need to push yourself a little more. I guarantee it gets easier the more you try, and each friend you make will help you to make more.

16 – 34

You are on the right path. Your charisma is there so don't hold back. Look for opportunities to use it more and prepare for astonishing results!

35 – 50

You must light up a room when you walk in! People feel your energy and are attracted to it. You have mastered how to win friends and influence people and the sky is the limit for the joy and success you can bring to yourself and others.

Summary

You may have been surprised to find you scored higher than you expected. That's because we all have charisma; as I said, we just see it in others before we see it in ourselves. Review the questions above to see which areas you aced and which ones you will want to improve.

Then, knowing where you want to make a change, use the following ten tips that relate to each question to improve your charisma until you start to see people lighting up whenever they see you.

1. The energy you project can determine the success of your connections. Here is where that big, sincere smile is so important. With that sparkle in your eyes and just being happy in the moment, you can usually grab almost anyone's attention. Who doesn't want to be around that person? You draw people to you because of your presence and energy, which rubs off on others. When you make others feel happy by being around you and communicating positive emotions, you will benefit and positively score more ACP points.

2. When meeting with a new person, no matter how different they may seem, take the time to ask questions to find common interests. Seek to discover their unique gifts. Someone once said that we come into this world to learn what it is we are to teach. Don't just ask what someone does; ask, "What is your passion?" At the very least, leave the conversation feeling fulfilled on some level. Even though it may not be an ideal client fit, it is a connection. A warm contact outranks a cold call any day of the week. If you take the time to

know them and make them feel special, you will be memorable. That's charisma!

3. To become a good conversationalist is to become a good listener. To be a good listener, you must care, really listen, and focus on what people have to say. There is a big difference between listening to and hearing someone. Charismatic people are empathetic. Sometimes people don't want an entertaining conversation partner, and they want someone who will listen to them. Make them feel like they are the only person in the room. Doing so is being kind. And it scores high marks in achieving a charismatic personality.

4. Charismatic people are comfortable in their skin and confident in who they are. They do not worry about what others might think or say about them if they speak openly. They do not seek validation from others and have a natural calmness about themselves.

5. If you are genuinely passionate about something like a belief or a cause, you will want to share it with everyone, and you will light up when you speak about it. You believe in it so much your energy around it is heightened. You will get people excited about it too, and they will support you or possibly get involved as long as you are consistent

with your message and actions. That is charisma.

6. People with charisma are great at telling stories; whether with humor or drama, they like to bring their audience on a journey that entertains while teaching. It is a special gift and scores high marks. If this is not one of your strongest areas, start to look at your days differently and find a story in each one. The stories are all around us, every day. Write the stories in a journal or maybe write a blog. This is a good way to build your storytelling muscle.

7. Being vulnerable is a good thing when it comes to charisma. Have you heard of The Pratfall Effect? In social psychology, the Pratfall Effect is the tendency for someone's interpersonal appeal to change after an individual makes a mistake, depending on the individual's perceived competence. When you admit to a mistake or a flaw, you become more likable, showing you are not perfect. Studies show that people connect to those who share their flaws. Take risks, be vulnerable, and be charismatic.

8. By being kind and non-judgmental, people are more likely to feel comfortable and trust you about discussing sensitive issues. The best is to understand. Instead of judging how someone looks or

acts, try to understand the person and be more accepting. This is where love comes in. As Walt Whitman said, "Be curious, not judgmental."

9. If your voice isn't powerful and confident, it may not reflect the expert you are. Here are some tips to consider: Control your volume, remember to pause when speaking, slow down your tempo, and absolutely do not allow an inflection at the end of sentences. Your voice is a reflection of who you are and naturally will attract your ideal clients. If your voice is reflecting the expert you, you naturally become magnetic. Here is where a voice coach can help.

10. Remembering people and their names is really important because their names connect to their identity and individuality, especially in new relationships. It makes people feel they matter and they made an impression on you, and that makes them feel good, and you should feel good too when that happens.

Charisma may appear to be a gift certain people possess or an inherent personality trait, but many behavioral scientists believe it can be learned. Some researchers say charisma comes down to how approachable you are or your likability, your ability to influence, and how you move to motivate others. Whatever the case, becoming more charismatic will open doors for you and lead to deeper and more fulfilling relationships.

If you would like a thirty-minute, no-obligation consultation by phone or Zoom to determine how I can help you, email me at anneg@annegarland-enterprises.com (put in subject line complimentary consultation). Or you can text me with your name and time zone at 860-575-4970.

Anne Garland

Anne Garland Enterprises, LLC
www.annegarlandenterprises.com
860-575-4970

ANNE'S PLAN-DO-REVIEW:

20 QUICK STEPS FOR A SUCCESSFUL NETWORKING EVENT

As an expert in event planning for corporate and creating and producing my personal events for more than thirty years, I get a lot of calls to help entrepreneurs.

One of my secrets to networking is hosting your own events where you are the star!

I have mastered bringing together both extroverts and introverts and creating a space for each type of person where they can network together with results.

While it can be a lot of work to create a networking event, it draws crowds, whether it is in-person or virtual. There are many considerations to its planning.

PLAN

1. Define your Purpose and Your Why

2. Who is your Target Market? Know your niche and whom you serve. (Hint: It's not everybody.)

3. Is this In-Person or Virtual?

4. Date, time, length of the event, consider holidays and conflicts.

5. In-Person: How many attendees?

6. Will you need team support? Who and how many?

7. In-Person: Select your location, venue, and food considerations.

8. Budget negotiations and contracts (There can be costs to virtual events.)

9. Program planning, speakers/handouts, vendors, sponsors, photographer.

10. Audiovisual requirements for both in-person and virtual.

DO

11. Graphics and social media marketing, FB group event page.

12. The registration process, before, and if in-person who, and the flow the day of the event.

13. Reminders for attendees, month, week, day of the event.

14. Day of event—serve your attendees. Everyone is a VIP!

15. Get testimonials day of the event! Live or written.

REVIEW

16. You did it! Congratulations! Honor YOU for your efforts.

17. Follow up with your team, attendees, vendors, and sponsors. (You can have virtual sponsors).

18. Promote photos on social media.

19. Review what worked and how it could be better.

20. Book your next event and keep the momentum going!

RESOURCES FOR DOWNLOAD

How Charismatic Are You? Take the Quiz

www.AnneGarlandEnterprises.com/charismatic-quiz

Anne's Plan-Do-Review: 20 Quick Steps for a Successful Event

www.AnneGarlandEnterprises.com/plan-do-review

The Connection Sales Incubator: Tracking Your Connections

www.AnneGarlandEnterprises.com/sales-incubator

Top 3 Mistakes Every Networker Must Avoid

www.AnneGarlandEnterprises.com/networking-no-nos

Top 10 Conversation Starters

www.AnneGarlandEnterprises.com/conversation-starters

ANNE'S LIST OF FAVORITE QUOTES
SECTION ONE

"Networking is about knowing more people. Connecting is about knowing people more."
— Author unknown

"Networking is the number one unwritten rule of success in business."
— Sally Krawcheck, author, power woman

"No one makes it alone."
— Anne Garland, author, speaker, master connector

"Networking is a lot like nutrition and fitness: we know what to do. The hard part is making it a top priority."
— Herminia Ibarra, professor, London Business School

"The opposite of networking is NOT working!"
— Someone Smart

"The richest people in the world look for and build networks. Everyone else looks for a job."

— Robert Kiyosaki, author of Rich Dad Poor Dad

Chapter 1

"You can make more friends in two months by becoming more interested in other people than you can in two years by trying to have them become interested in you."

— Dale Carnegie, American writer, lecturer

Chapter 2

"Oh, the places you'll go!"

— Dr. Seuss, children's author

Chapter 3

"Call it a clan, call it a network, call it a tribe, call it a family; whatever you call it, whoever you are, you need one."

— Jane Howard, author

Chapter 4

"Begin with the end in mind."

— Franklin Covey, author

Chapter 5

"Efforts and courage are not enough without purpose and direction."

— President John F. Kennedy

Chapter 6

"Let the light of your presence illuminate every room you enter."

— Wayne Gerard Trotman, British independent filmmaker

Chapter 7

"There is so much we can do to render service, to make a difference in the world—no matter how large or small our circle of influence."

— Stephen Covey, author

Chapter 8

"A simple hello could lead to a million things."

— Nicola Jones-Crossley, writer, researcher, business consultant

Chapter 9

"Look at questions as keys on a keyring. Questions unlock doors. The bigger your keyring the more keys you have, the more doors you can unlock."

— John C. Maxwell, author, speaker, pastor

Chapter 10

"Opportunities are like sunrises. If you wait too long you will miss them."

— William Arthur Ward, motivational writer

Chapter 11

"Everything you do now is your future."

— Author unknown

Chapter 12

"Those who win in networking give first, give generously, and give often."

— Author unknown

SECTION TWO

"The power of visibility can never be underestimated."

— Margaret Cho, comedian

Chapter 13

"Ninety-nine percent of success is showing up, even virtually."

— Anne Garland, author, speaker, master connector

Chapter 14

"I like to connect with people in the virtual world, exchanging thoughts and ideas, when in the physical world we might never have the opportunity to cross paths."

— Demi Moore, actress

Chapter 15

"Technology is nothing. What's important is that you have a faith in people, that they're basically good and smart, and if you give them tools, they'll do wonderful things with them."

— Steve Jobs, American inventor, designer, and entrepreneur

Chapter 16

"Body language is a very powerful tool. We had body language before we had speech, and apparently, 80 percent of what you understand in a conversation is read through the body, not the words."

— Deborah Bull, British dancer

Chapter 17

"Your personal brand is a promise to your clients…a promise of quality, consistency, competency, and reliability."

— Jason Hartman, Founder and CEO of the Hartman Media Company

Chapter 18

"Any virtual community that works, works because people put in some time."

— Howard Rheingold, American critic

Chapter 19

"It takes months to find a customer and minutes to lose one."

— Renee Evenson, author

Chapter 20

"The hilarious thing about people working from home is when their work is done, they say, 'Let's go home.' Then they realize, they are already at home."

— Author unknown

SECTION THREE

"Desire is the key to motivation, but it's determination and commitment to an unrelenting pursuit of your goal—a commitment to excellence—that will enable you to attain the success you seek."

— Mario Andretti, Indy 500 racing driver

Chapter 21

"An event is not over until everyone is tired of talking about it."

— Mason Cooley, American aphorist

Chapter 22

"An archer cannot hit the bull's eye if he doesn't know where the target is."

— Author unknown

Chapter 23

"Day, n. A period of twenty-four hours, mostly misspent."

— Ambrose Bierce, American short story writer

Chapter 24

"Nothing can cure the soul but the senses just as nothing can cure the senses but the soul."

— Oscar Wilde, Irish writer and poet

Chapter 25

"The value of networking is not measured by the number of people we meet but by the number of people we introduce to others."

— Simon Sinek, author and inspirational speaker

Chapter 26

"The intense happiness of our union is derived in a high degree from the perfect freedom with which we follow and declare our happiness."

— T. S. Eliot, poet, essayist

Chapter 27

"Success is not a destination. It's a journey."

— Zig Ziglar, American motivational speaker

344 SECRETS OF A SERIAL NETWORKER

Chapter 28

"First comes thought; then organization of that thought, into idea and plans; then transformation of those plans into reality. The beginning as you will observe, is in your imagination."

— Napoleon Hill, American author

Chapter 29

"Magic is believing in yourself. If you can do that, you can make anything happen."

— Johann Wolfgang von Goethe, German poet, playwright, novelist

Chapter 30

"Whatever you do, do it well. Do it so well that when people see you do it, they will want to come back and see you do it again, and they will want to bring others and show them how well you do what you do."

— Walt Disney, American entrepreneur, animator, writer, voice actor, film producer

A Final Note

"The currency of real networking is not greed but generosity."

— Keith Ferrazzi, American author

ANNE'S "A LIST" OF VIP RESOURCES

As a Serial Networker with many contacts and connections, I am highlighting a few people who have been mentioned in *Secrets of a Serial Networker* as resources for you, should you choose.

I have listed each person as they appear in the book and their information as of the Publishing date 2.2.22.

Terra Bohlmann, Business Coach for Women Entrepreneurs, Houston, TX | www.TerraBohlmann.com

Mary Carangelo, Stylist and Fashion Therapist, West Hartford, CT | www.MCStyling.com

Chala Dincoy, One-On-One Marketing Coach, Toronto, Canada | www.GroYourBiz.com

Susan Epstein, Business Coach, Mastermind Expert, and Author, New London, CT | www.Highly-ProfitablePractice.com

Janine James, Founding Solutionist and Creative Director | www.ImaginetheNext.com

Monique McDonald, Voice Specialist and Charismatic Coach, The Magnetic Voice, NYC | www.

MagneticVoice.com

Deborah Stuart, President and Founder of High Chi Energy Jewelry, Sausalito, CA | www.HighChi.com

Diane Trone, Certified Stylist, Owner of The Blonde Hanger & His Hanger Boutique, Stonington, CT | www.BlondeHanger.com

Sally Tucker, Coldwell Banker Realty, Award-Winning Realtor, Branford, CT | www.Sally-Tucker.com

Elaine Williams, Vocal Coach, Speaker Coach, Author, Comedian, NJ | Text 646-526-3522

Sandra Yancey, CEO and Founder, eWomenNetwork, Dallas, TX | www.eWomenNetwork.com

ABOUT SPOTLIGHT COACHING

DO NOT WASTE ANOTHER MOMENT (OR DIME) ON NETWORKING UNTIL YOU READ THIS!

Are you a entrepreneur who is:

- Discouraged by the lack of response for your networking efforts? Unsure how to best go about making the right connections?

- Leery of the overly "sales-y" networking tactics that feel uncomfortable and so not you?

- Terrified that you'll have to give up on your dream of business ownership and settle into many more years of a ho-hum soul-sucking JOB?

- The good news is that through better networking building, a successful business is within your reach!

Up until now, you likely just didn't have the confidence and know-how to make your networking work for you. That changes today!

You can master networking that causes your ideal clients to stop in their tracks and listen to your message!

You can discover the best networking techniques to

351

deliver maximum results into your business.

You can master networking that is authentic and gen-uine...no trickery or sleazy sales tactics required!

You can start connecting with people who are excited to meet you, to work with you, and to pay you.

You can start serving the people who need you most!

It all starts today.

Your success begins with a simple phone call or text. Please contact me to request a no-charge Busi-ness Success Networking Evaluation. During this fif-teen-minute phone consultation, we'll evaluate your business goals, determine if you're on the right path to your version of networking success, and identify resources that can help you reach your goals much more quickly than you thought possible!

Please call or text (860) 575-4970
to schedule a complimentary phone conversation
with me and find out if you're on the right path to
business success—and where a few tweaks could
help you reach your goals much quicker than you
thought possible!

www.AnneGarlandEnterprises.com/coaching

ABOUT WING WOMAN COACHING

Does this sound like you?

You want to network, but the thought of "flying solo" at a networking event terrifies you. Are you unsure where to go, whom to approach, and what to say when you do?

What if you could be coached on the spot with me as your Wing Woman?

This one-of-a-kind, stand-alone program is a great way to learn how to effectively network alongside a networking expert. Contact me for more details.

Please call or text (860) 575-4970 to schedule a complimentary phone conversation with me and find out if this is for you.

www.AnneGarlandEnterprises.com/coaching

ABOUT THE AUTHOR

ANNE GARLAND (pronounced "Annie") is an author, professional speaker, serial networker, professional coach, intuitive connector, event producer, and empowerment entrepreneur. She thrives on connecting people who, together, can produce real and rewarding results.

She is a catalyst for creativity, self-development, and sales. Using the power of shared spaces and places, she engages and connects the right people at the right time, allowing them to reach their goals faster than they thought possible.

By leveraging her years of global marketing and sales experience, Anne taps into a vast resume that includes working for top international brands like BASF, Honeywell, Hanes, and others. Her keen sense of interior design creativeness—honed by working with commercial architects, delivers a one-two combination of creative strategies. This knocks out the competition and brings out the best in people and teams.

Today, Anne celebrates the fact that her networking events have had a dazzling effect on so many for more than thirty-five years. A natural networker, she discovered her gift for resourcefulness at the age of ten when she sold ninety boxes of Girl Scout Cookies by calling her brother's paper route customers for orders. She was fearless and had no idea then that her first corporate job was to be a long-distance telephone operator and that eventually sales or the term "networking" would become a major part of her life's passion and legacy. She did what felt natural and outsold the next highest cookie seller by seventy-five boxes!

Anne has co-authored two books, including the Amazon bestseller Be the Beacon and Make Your Connections Count. Secrets of a Serial Networker is her first solo book.

Anne and her husband Keith share sacred space with their two seventy-five-pound collies, Duke and Duchess, splitting time between their fifty-acre-wood rural Connecticut home and their summer beach house in Old Lyme. In addition, they enjoy frequent visits with their adult children and beloved five grandchildren. Keith and Anne love sports cars and riding their motorcycle through the back roads, viewing parts of Connecticut rarely seen from a car.

ABOUT ANNE GARLAND ENTERPRISES, LLC

How It All Began

GIRLS' GOALS AT THE GRIS

In the early 2000s, during an informal girls' holiday recovery lunch at the Griswold Inn, Essex, Connecticut, I asked each of the five women present to write out their year-long goals. No one seemed to take me seriously and they called the waiter over for more drinks. Six months later, I ran into Sandy Smith, who had attended the lunch; she hugged me and said, "Thank you. Because of you and the goal exercise we did in January, I published my book!" Excited, she continued to say, "I hope we can do it again this year." I was gobsmacked! I thought more about the event and decided to reach out to a few more ladies and offer it again. It grew to twelve. The following year it grew to twenty, then thirty, and continued to grow each year. All of this was while I was working my corporate job.

In 2022, I celebrated my twentieth anniversary of what is now known as Girls' Goals at the Gris, hosting sixty-five women (that is all the space can hold) for a post-holiday recovery event on the third Saturday in January. We never missed a celebration due to New England weather. However, in 2021, we were able to invite thirty ladies for a safe event. The restaurant was opening its doors again to the public after being closed for so long due to the pandemic.

In 2022, I rebranded Girls' Goals at the Gris (GGG) to Girls Gathering at the Gris.

THE IDEA CIRCLE FOR WOMEN

While I continued working corporate and traveling, I would often host gatherings for women offering different events. I enlisted my Board of Directors, which led to idea-sharing and ongoing mutual support that became the genesis and vision to create inspirational events and workshops I branded "The Idea Circle for Women."

In 2008, I made the final decision to leave the corporate job market, having been laid off the third consecutive year due to corporate mergers and acquisitions. That was three jobs in three years! That is when Anne Garland Enterprises, LLC was formed, and I was on my own creating and producing my own events.

I began creating and producing unique programs for women who wanted to enhance their lives while seeking connections with like-minded women having fun! At the same time, I featured various local experts, giving them a platform to be seen on center stage.

That year I connected with one of my gal pals, Nancy Ottino, a twin flame, and together we collaborated to produce a major conference for women. It took a year of planning and was a success. Upon its closing, Nancy decided she didn't want to continue with the conferences, but I did, and for four more years, it became my annual main event, called The Idea Circle for Women. I also held smaller events throughout the years under that brand.

All of my events until 2020 were branded under The Idea Circle for Women. Today, I brand everything under Anne Garland Enterprises; however, I have not formally retired The Idea Circle for Women. People still relate to this brand.

SPEAKER MASTERY SERIES

This is a virtual monthly program where I bring one to three experts together with a specific topic.

3 Masters | 1 Session | 90 Minutes of Pure Power

1 Master | 1 Session | 30 Minutes of Pure Power

SENSATIONAL SCHMOOZE

Cocktails/Courses and Clever Conversations

Remarkable women have a rare opportunity to share in an extraordinary networking event unlike anything they have experienced before. The evening includes one of the most unique dining experiences because you share one of four plate courses, each with a different partner with a twist. Expect other fun surprises to get you connected at a deeper level to each of your four table partners.

Limited to 40 | Annual Event held in Eastern Connecticut

SUCCESS MASTERMIND

Why My Mastermind Group Can Accelerate Your Success

What if I told you that you can put yourself in a better position to succeed by simply sharing your time, either once a week or once a month, with other like-minded and motivated individuals?

My mastermind is a peer-mentoring group of individuals who meet on a regular basis (in-person or virtually) to push each other to work to their highest potential and hold each other accountable.

These are the six reasons it benefits you and your business:

1. **Accountability:** In our group, we have myself and accountability buddies who will keep you accountable. Powerful and deeper connections are made with this process.

2. **Feedback:** The people in our group can be your best source of advice at times when you're unsure where to turn.

3. **Collaboration:** Not only does our mastermind group allow you to collaborate on ideas, but you can help people or get people in our group to help you with projects or tasks.

4. **Network:** Having connections and knowing people who might know people in various industries can come in handy when you least expect it.

5. **Resourceful:** The blending of different backgrounds, skills, and knowledge of our women creates a fantastic environment for you to learn, play off of your strengths, and correct your weaknesses

6. **Support:** Every week in my mastermind, someone is blown away by the quality of help and solutions they receive to their problems. It never ceases to amaze me how creative we can get, as a group,

to tackle someone's issues in that meeting. Powerful!

This program when available may be both virtual and in-person.

ANNE GARLAND ENTERPRISES SUPPORTS COMMUNITY

Giving back has always been a part of my events, including a local women's nonprofit receiving donations or a percentage of the proceeds. As often happens when I create a safe space for women to connect in a fun format with unique content, they leave inspired and energized. But, ultimately, I am the one whose heart and soul are fulfilled.

Anne Garland Enterprises, LLC is the umbrella for all of my events, including:

- Chic Club VIP
- Girls' Goals at the Gris
- Girls Gathering at the Gris
- Idea Circle for Women
- Mastery Series
- Sensational Schmooze
- Success Mastermind

BOOK ANNE GARLAND TO SPEAK AT YOUR NEXT EVENT

Meet Anne Garland (pronounced Annie).

Anne is an author, professional speaker, professional coach, strategist, serial networker, intuitive connector, event producer, and empowerment entrepreneur.

You've heard of Six Degrees of Separation? Anne Garland can cut that down to one. Anne is the ultimate connector and has been since her early career at the telephone company. In a world where who you know can be more powerful than what you know, Anne knows how to bring the right people together to produce bold, positive results.

Anne taps into a vast resume that includes working for top international brands like BASF, Honeywell, Hanes, Nanotex. and others. That background coupled with her years of architectural interior design expertise delivers a one-two combination of creative strategies that allows her to bring out the best in individuals and teams. Her experiential networking events have been dazzling people for over thirty years.

As an award-winning presenter and event producer, Anne makes it her mission to inspire others. Passionate about inspiring mostly women entrepreneurs, and a few good men, her goal is to motivate them to move from the sidelines to center stage.

Credits:

- National Speakers Association,(NSA-CT) President, Connecticut Chapter 2020-2021
- eWomenNetwork, (eWN) Executive Managing Director 2013-2017
- American Society of Interior Designers,(ASID) President, Connecticut Chapter 2004-2005

If you would like a complimentary, no-obligation thirty-minute consultation by phone, or Zoom to determine how I can help you gain more confidence networking, email me at anneg@annegarlandenterprises.com or text me with your name and time zone at (860) 575-4970 to set up your complimentary consultation.